Test Your Business English

J. S. McKellen

Illustrated by Robin Harris
and Ross Thomson

PENGUIN ENGLISH

PENGUIN ENGLISH

Published by the Penguin Group
Penguin Books Ltd, 27 Wrights Lane, London W8 5TZ, England
Penguin Books USA Inc., 375 Hudson Street, New York, New York 10014, USA
Penguin Books Australia Ltd, Ringwood, Victoria, Australia
Penguin Books Canada Ltd, 10 Alcorn Avenue, Toronto, Ontario, Canada M4V 3B2
Penguin Books (NZ) Ltd, 182–190 Wairau Road, Auckland 10, New Zealand

Penguin Books Ltd, Registered Offices: Harmondsworth, Middlesex, England

First published 1990
10 9 8 7 6 5 4

Filmset in Century Schoolbook

Printed and bound in Great Britain by
BPCC Hazells Ltd
Member of BPCC Ltd

INTRODUCTION

Since English is the international language of business, a knowledge of English business terms is essential for successful business people, even if their main function is not in international trade. This book, part of the *Test Your Vocabulary* series, is designed to help the reader to acquire this knowledge.

The choice of which language items to include has been made on a practical basis: how often the words are used, and how important it is to know them. Informal (and, in one instance, spoken) language is included, with tests of appropriacy in register; some words appear in more than one context. The areas of business covered range from basic office practice to specialised areas such as import/export and insurance.

A range of exercise types, including gap-filling, multiple choice, dialogue completion, crosswords, anagrams, etc., is provided to stimulate and help the reader to internalise the vocabulary.

TO THE STUDENT

You will not necessarily wish or need to test yourself in all the areas of business covered in this book. But in order for the new words to become "fixed" in your mind, you need to test yourself again and again. We suggest that you:

1 Read the instructions carefully and try the test (writing your answers **in pencil** and checking them).
2 Correct any mistakes and pay special attention to words which caused you difficulty or that you got wrong.
3 Wait five or ten minutes, then try the test again. (Cover your answers or get a friend to read out the questions.)
4 Repeat this until you know all the words.
5 Now **rub out your answers** and try the test again the next day; again, pay special attention to any words which cause difficulty.
6 Make sure that you try the test again at least twice within the next month; this should "fix" most of the words in your mind.

ACKNOWLEDGEMENTS

I owe a debt of gratitude to Peter Watcyn-Jones, who devised the *Test Your Vocabulary* series, and whose Advice to the Student is used, almost unchanged, here. He has read the final manuscript and made many helpful suggestions. I also owe a particular debt of thanks to Jake Allsop, who has commented in detail on every test and has improved most immensely. (Any remaining mistakes are my own.)

CONTENTS

In the office

In the office

Choosing from the words in the box, write the numbers of the items in the labels. The first has been done for you.

1 paper-clips	5 waste-paper basket	9 door
2 calculator	6 filing cabinet	10 desk diary
3 file	7 headed paper	11 coat stand
4 stapler	8 notebook	12 shelf

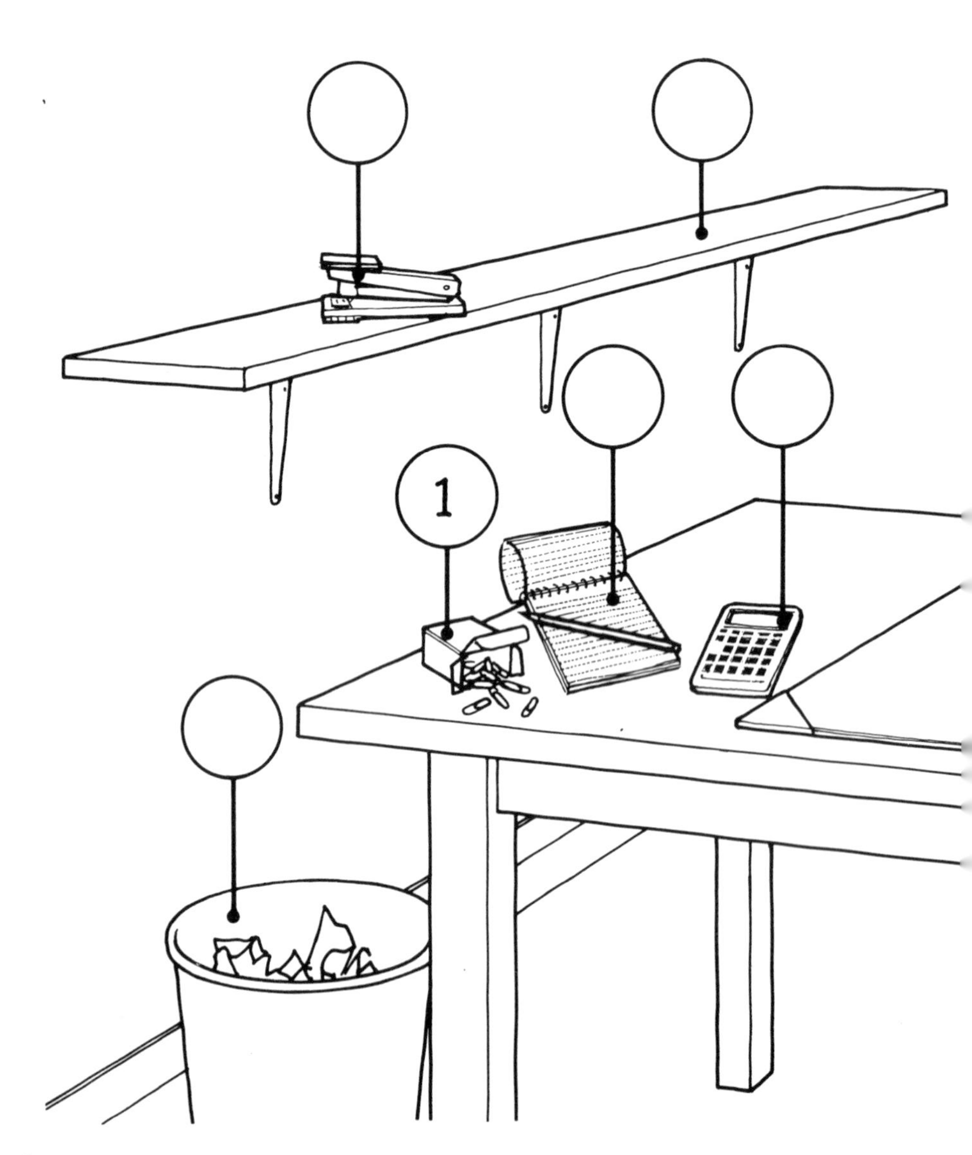

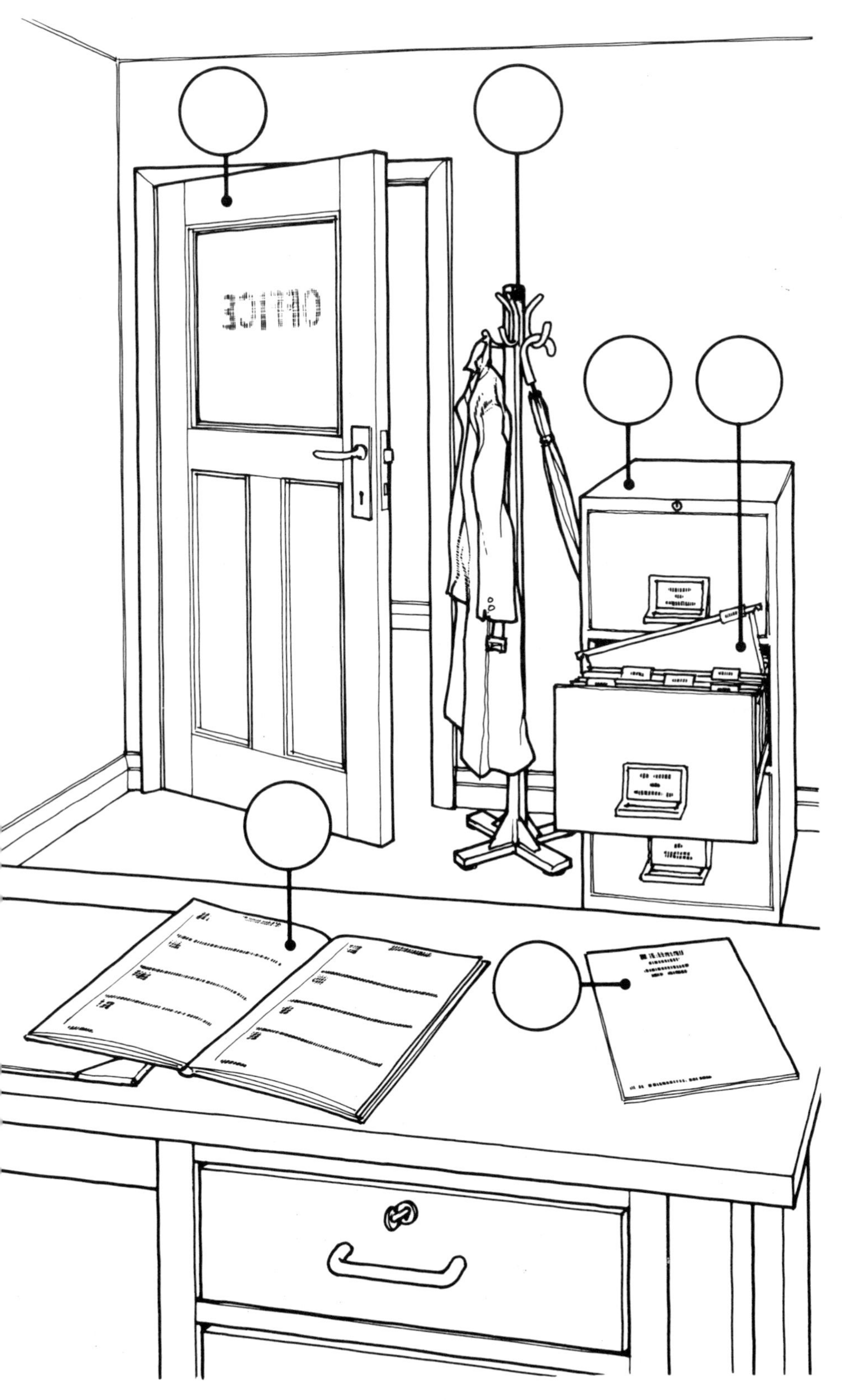

Secretarial duties 1

Complete this letter from Jane, a young secretary just starting her first job, to her friend Susan. Choose from the words in the box to fill in the gaps. The first has been done for you.

shorthand	notebook	screen
minutes	post book	word processor
memos	proof reading	letters
petty cash	audio typing	typewriter
diary	typing	

Dear Susan,

Well, I've got the job! and I seem to need most of the things I learned in College.

They wanted to know my (1) **shorthand** and (2) .... speeds, and what kind of a (3) .... I was used to, and whether I could use a (4) .... as well. Because my boss, Mr Sutherland, is away from the office a lot he often dictates on to a cassette tape, so they wanted to know if I could manage (5) .... But they also gave me a shorthand (6) .... They explained that I will often be making appointments for Mr Sutherland, so I must keep his (7) .... I'll also be typing his correspondence and when he is away I may have to sign some of his (8) .... I'll also be responsible for circulating (9) .... to other members of the staff, and when I go to meetings I'll be taking the (10) .... Because I'll be buying the stamps and coffee and so on, I'll deal with the (11) .... and keep the (12) .... They also want me to (13) .... callers to the office, so that Mr Sutherland doesn't get disturbed when he's busy. And I'll have to do some (14) .... (of catalogues, press releases, and things like that). So I think I'll keep busy!

It all sounds fascinating, and I'm terribly excited!

Love,

Jane

Secretarial duties 2

Jane wrote to Susan after her first week at work. Complete the letter. Choose from the words in the box to fill in the gaps. The first has been done for you.

travel agents	directory enquiries
previous correspondence	circulation
system	index
responsibility	reference
personal assistant	job
travel arrangements	international telephone operator

Dear Susan,

Well, I've been working for a week, and I must say I'm still bewildered. I hope it all sorts itself out.

Mr Sutherland is going away on a business trip – isn't it exciting? He's going to Spain, Portugal and Italy.

The first thing I had to do was to make his (1) **travel** **arrangements** so I had to talk to the (2) .... the Company uses and get them to book all the trains, planes and hotels, and I also had to organise his car hire, make the appointments and fix up his meetings. I've used the telephone a lot. The (3) .... has got quite used to my voice, and the lady who deals with (4) .... must be quite tired of me! I also had to look up the (5) .... he's had with the people he'll be seeing, and sort out the letters he'll need to take with him.

We organised the (6) .... list for memos. (He'll be sending tapes back to me.) While he's away, I've promised to reorganise his filing (7) .... and make up an (8) .... to the files, so that he can find things quickly. I've also got to learn which (9) .... books to use when I need to find something!

By the time I've done all this, I'll be really pleased with my (10) ....! I'm really going to be a real secretary, not just a shorthand typist; in fact I'm nearly a (11) .... – P.A. for short – as I do take complete (12) .... for some areas of the work.

See you soon!

Jane

Secretarial work

Look at the pictures. The captions below each picture are incomplete. Choose from the words in the box to complete each. The first has been done for you.

w.p.m. (words per minute)	diary	dictation
shorthand	franking machine	post book
confidential secretary	word processor	petty cash
		training

1 I'm ready to take your **dictation** now.

2 I'm sorry, Mr Jones, but could you go a little more slowly? My .... isn't good enough to keep up with you.

3 I've got lots to do. Isn't it lucky my typing speed is 50 ....?

4 Yes, I've had a year's .... at the Loamshire Secretarial College.

5 Yes, I think Tuesday at 3 o'clock will be O.K., but let me just check my ....

6 You must always record the letters. Let's find the ....

7 I've run out of stamps. Can I use the .... to buy some more, please?

8 That's his .... She never says anything about what goes on in his office.

9 Life's much better now we've got this .... and don't have to stick on all those stamps, isn't it?

10 Yes, and I can get through three times as much work with the .... as I could with a typewriter.

Numbers

How would you say these numbers? Write them in words.

1 12,402
2 1,001,111
3 21
4 .15
5 .002
6 ¼
7 ½
8 ⅓

What are these numbers in figures? Write them.

9 one million seven hundred and fifty-four thousand three hundred and twenty-one
10 one billion
11 ninety-two
12 three thousand four hundred and two
13 one hundred and ninety nine point nine recurring
14 point nought two
15 one point eight

What is the answer to these sums? Write the sums and the answers in figures. (Note: K = 1000; m = million.)

16 twelve times eight
17 thirty eight times two
18 one hundred and forty four divided by twelve
19 eight times fifty K
20 three times one point five m.

6 Communications

Some of the following sentences are true, but some are false. Tick (√) the correct box. The first one has been done for you.

		T	F
1	Fax machines require a different kind of telephone.		
2	A fax is a facsimile of the original, and looks exactly like it.		
3	A company can only have a telex number if it subscribes to the service.		
4	Telegrams can be sent from one person to another inside the UK.		
5	The telegram service between the UK and the USA has been discontinued.		
6	Most countries can now be telephoned without the help of the operator.		
7	Charges for all telephone calls are the same whether they are made during the day or the night.		
8	Hotels often charge a surcharge for handling telephone calls through the hotel switchboard.		
9	Each country that can be reached by direct dialling has its own code.		
10	The code for a city or town is the same whether it is dialled from within a country or from another country.		
11	International telephone operators are required by law to speak English.		
12	The postcode used in the UK is the equivalent of the zipcode used in the USA.		
13	A county in Britain is of the same importance as a county in the USA.		
14	English abbreviations in telexes are internationally recognised.		

Travel

Label the illustrations, choosing from the words in the box. The first has been done for you.

a check-in desk	**e** single room	**i** private bath
b reception desk	**f** double room	**j** check-out time
c twin-bedded double room	**g** flight number	**k** departure time
d boarding pass	**h** ticket	**l** departure lounge

1 a check-in desk

2

3

4

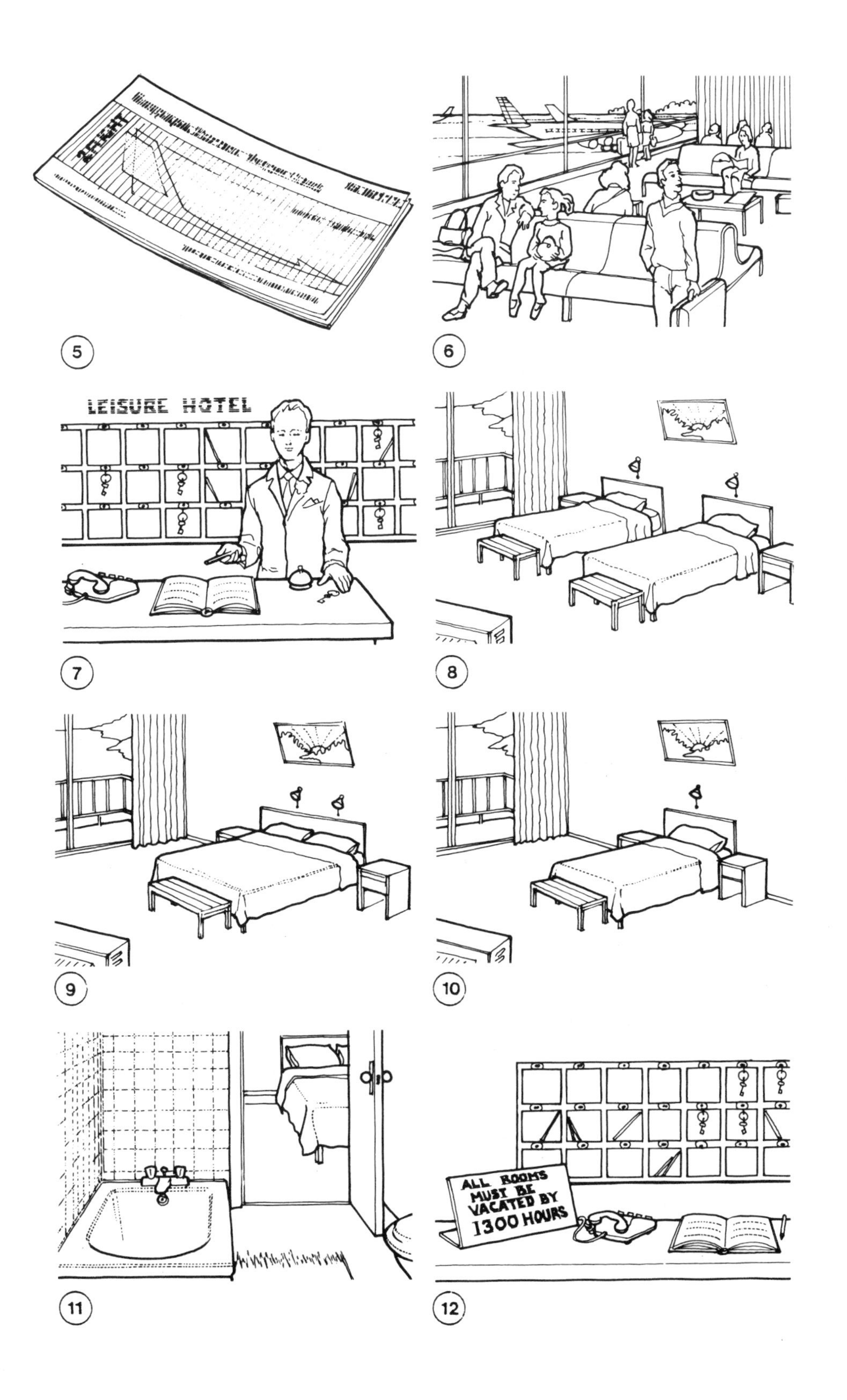

5
6
7
8
9
10
11
12

8 Business letters 1

Choosing from the words in the box, label the parts of the letter. The first has been done for you.

date	main paragraph	letterhead
references	salutation	introductory paragraph
concluding paragraph	recipient's address	(sender's) address
(typed) signature	complimentary ending	enclosures (abbreviation)
position/title	signature	

(1) WIDGETRY LTD

6 Pine Estate, Westhornet, Bedfordshire, UB18 22BC.

(2) Telephone 9017 23456 Telex X238 WID Fax 9017 67893

(3) Michael Scott, Sales Manager,
Smith and Brown plc,
Napier House,
North Molton Street,
Oxbridge OB84 9TD.

(4) Your ref. MS/WID/15/88
Our ref. ST/MN/10/88

(5) 31 January 19––

(6) Dear Mr Scott,

(7) Thank you for your letter of 20 January, explaining that the super widgets, catalogue reference X-3908, are no longer available but that ST-1432, made to the same specifications but using a slightly different alloy, are now available instead.

(8) Before I place a firm order I should like to see samples of the new super widgets. If the replacement is as good as you say it is, I shall certainly wish to reinstate the original order, but placing an order for the new items. Apart from anything else, I should prefer to continue to deal with Smith and Brown, whose service has always been satisfactory in the past. But you will understand that I must safeguard Widgetry's interests and make sure that the quality is good.

(9) I would, therefore, be grateful if you could let me have a sample as soon as possible.

(10) Yours sincerely,

(11) Simon Thomas

(12) Simon Thomas
(13) Production Manager

(14) enc.

Business letters 2

This second letter has been revised so many times by Mr Thomas that it has become all mixed up, and his word processor has failed to reorganise it. Arrange the letter so that everything is in the right place. The first point in the letter is:

(2) **WIDGETRY LTD**

(1) Simon Thomas

(2) WIDGETRY LTD

(3) 6 Pine Estate, Westhornet, Bedfordshire, UB18 22BC
Telephone 9017 23456 Telex X238 WID Fax 9017 67893

(4) I look forward to hearing from you.

(5) Your ref. MS/WD/22/88
Our ref. JB/MS/48/88

(6) Yours sincerely,

(7) James Bowers, Sales Manager,
Electroscan Ltd,
Orchard Road Estate,
Oxbridge UB84 10SF.

(8) Production Manager

(9) Thank you for your letter. I am afraid that we have a problem with your order.

(10) 6 June 19– –

(11) Unfortunately, the manufacturers of the part you wish to order have advised us that they cannot supply it until September. Would you prefer
us to supply a substitute, or would you rather wait until the original parts are again available?

(12) Dear Mr Bowers

10 Taking the minutes

These are the minutes of a meeting. Some parts have been left out. Choosing from the words in the box, complete the minutes. The first has been done for you.

Minutes of the last meeting	Present	chairman
Any Other Business	chaired	Members
subcommittee	Seconder	Apologies
Date of next meeting	Proposer	Action

(1) **Present**...: Mr Jones (chairman) Ms Perkins Ms Carson
Mr Smith Ms Trueman (secretary)

(2) ....: Ms Green and Mr Brown were unable to attend and sent their apologies

(3) ....: No business remained from the last meeting.

Membership of the Committee

It was agreed that the Production Manager should be invited to become a member of this Committee.

Proposer: Ms Perkins
(4) ....: Mr Smith
Carried unanimously

1992: Development of European markets

A (5) .... is to be set up to consider ways in which the company can meet the challenge. (6) .... should be drawn from the Sales, Publicity and Marketing departments; Mr Jones will be the (7) .... of this.

Other developments

After some discussion, it was agreed that Ms Perkins should look into the possibilities of moving some manufacturing operations to Kenya.

(8) .... : Mr Jones
Seconder: Ms Carson
Carried unanimously

Next year's promotional budget

The heads of the Design, Promotion, Sales and Marketing Departments are to form a committee to work on this. The committee will be (9) .... by Mr Jones and he will notify the people concerned.

(10) ....: Mr Jones

(11) ....: Since there was nothing further, the meeting was adjourned.

(12) ....: The next meeting will be held on 6th March.

11 Computers 1

Choosing from the words in the box, write the numbers of the items in the labels. The first has been done for you.

1 keyboard	**4** screen	**7** printout	**10** disk storage box
2 monitor	**5** printer	**8** operator	**11** display
3 disk drive	**6** mouse	**9** disk	**12** modem

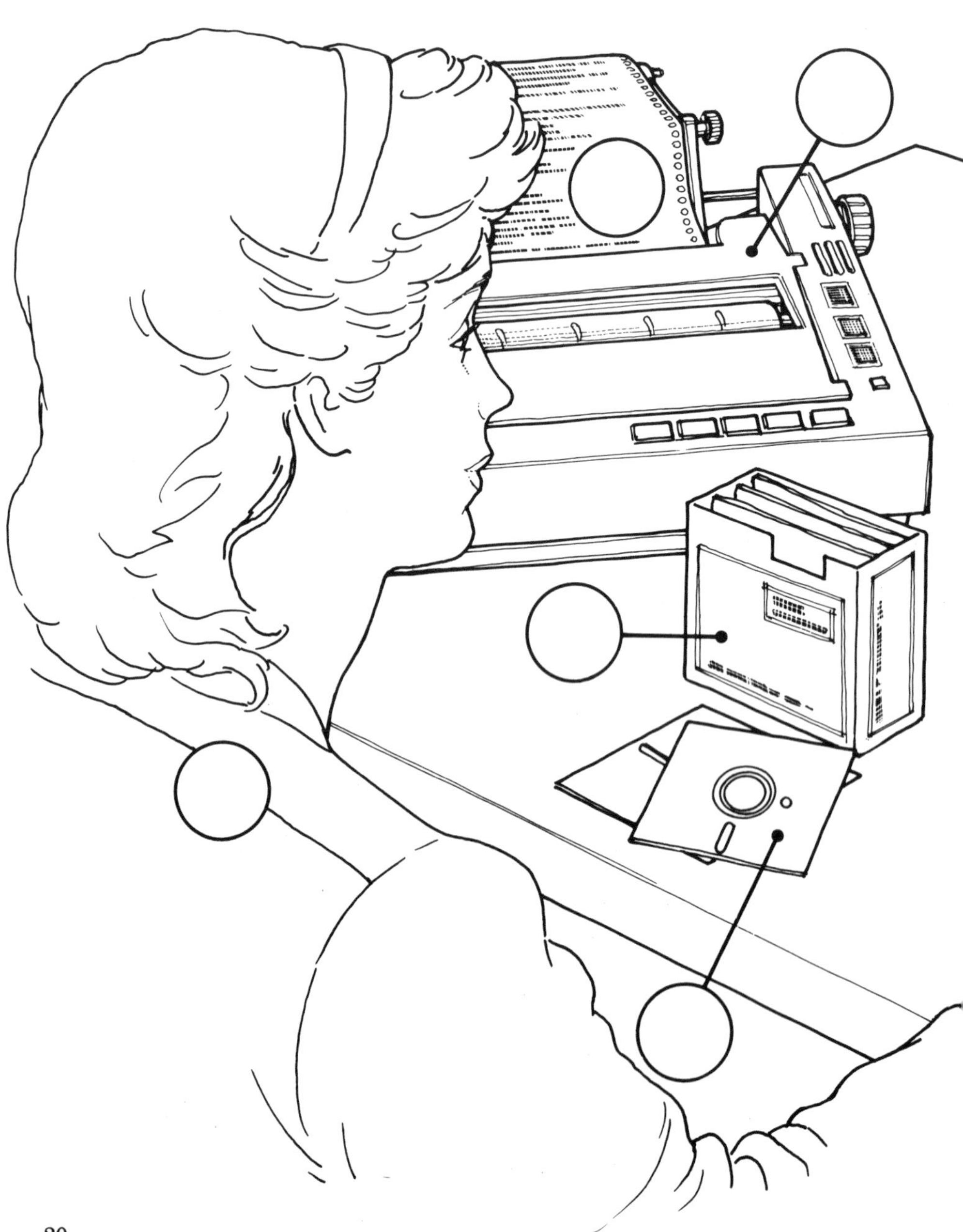

1

Computers 2

PART A

Choosing from the words in the box, fill in the words in the sentences. The first has been done for you. The figures in brackets ( ) show the number of letters in the word.

information	chips	WYSIWYG	controls
processing	RAM	graphics	systems
load	ROM	bugs	scroll
files			

1 Problems in programs are caused by ....**bugs**..... (4).

2 Silicon .... (5) contain a set of integrated circuits, reduced to a very small size.

3 Obtaining .... (11) is done by .... (10) data.

4 Software produces images which can appear on the screen as .... (8).

5 Memory that is permanent, cannot be written to, and can only be read, is .... (3).

6 Memory into which information can be loaded and from which data can be read, is .... (3).

7 Operators .... (4) into the computer's memory a program that they want to use.

8 Analysing ways of doing things, and of improving them, is done by .... (7) analysts.

9 "What you see is what you get" explains .... (7).

10 A single disk can contain a large number of different .... (5).

11 .... (8) can carry out instructions or operations when certain conditions occur.

12 The operators .... (6) lines of text up the screen, so that a new line appears at the bottom and the top line disappears.

PART B

Now find the words in the square. They may run from left to right, from top to bottom, or from bottom to top. One example has been done to help you.

P	C	H	I	P	S	E	F	U	L	P
R	O	O	P	R	Z	I	I	H	D	N
O	N	K	U	O	F	T	L	R	A	O
C	T	Y	R	O	M	S	E	R	P	I
E	R	W	F	E	Q	I	S	O	L	T
S	O	N	S	Y	S	T	E	M	S	A
S	L	W	Y	S	I	W	Y	G	T	M
I	S	P	L	I	C	D	B	R	A	R
N	L	A	E	T	R	O	M	A	H	O
G	L	P	R	G	T	U	E	P	V	F
N	O	M	B	I	D	N	T	H	S	N
X	R	A	U	L	A	M	L	I	S	I
Y	C	R	G	R	O	I	P	C	N	A
Z	S	L	S	U	L	P	U	S	T	X

13 Computers 3

Complete the passage below, choosing your words from the box. The first has been done for you.

hardware	saved
programs	personal computers
desktop publishing programs	software
retrieved	graphics
network	IBM compatible
spreadsheets	word processing
communications programs	accounting programs
keys in/types in	database management programs
mainframe computer	

Computer (1) **hardware** consists of a computer, a monitor, a keyboard, a printer, and their connections. The (2) .... contains the various (3) .... you run on your computer. The most common programs used in business are those for (4) .... (writing letters, documents, etc.), (5) .... (for budgets and financial analysis), (6) .... (for keeping names and addresses of customers), (7) .... (for book-keeping), (8) .... programs (for drawing charts, etc.), (9) .... (for electronic mail), and (10) .... (for producing manuals, catalogues, etc.). The operator (11) .... the information which can be (12) .... and (13) .... at a later date.

Most businesses nowadays use (14) ...., or PCs, which are often linked together in a local (15) .... This is a big change from the days when time had to be rented on a (16) .... Nowadays these are only used by very large businesses, universities, or Government departments. The two most popular types of computers currently are those of IBM and Apple (the Macintosh). It was IBM who set the standard for the PC which others later imitated. That is why, in order to be able to use the widest range of software, a computer has to be (17) ....

Companies and management

The art of management

Read the text. Then read the clues and complete the crossword. All the words can be found in the text, and one has been done for you. The numbers in brackets ( ) show how many letters there are in the word.

Each department in a division of a company relies on budgeting to make the company's affairs profitable. A profit target is set, and the unit price of the goods (which depends on how much they cost to make and for how much they can be sold) is determined by this; the managers report how well this target has been met; the price of the goods leaving the factory (or ex works) is adjusted. Only after this has been done can the various departments in the company execute the orders.

Many businesses fail because they fall into the trap of ignoring their cash-flow, often because they allow too generous credit terms. The accounts department should make sure that a stop is put on the credit granted to bad payers. The smooth running of the company depends on a good relationship between the boss and the people who work on the shop-floor.

Senior managers, of course, must pass some of their tasks over to other people – they simply cannot do it all. This delegation of some jobs is essential, and the ability to do it well is one of the measures of good management.

ACROSS

1 This depends on production costs, profit margins, and market sensitivity (5)
3 The cost of each item (4)
4 Word used for everything a company does (7)
5 The price of the goods depends on the .... (4) of their production
8 A good manager is good at this; he does not try to do everything himself (10)
10 Price of goods ....-factory (2)
12 To withdraw credit (4)
13 Something which is aimed at (6)

DOWN

1 Not only must a company make money, it must be .... (10)
2 Each .... (8) will usually have a senior manager and be organised in its own way
6 Smaller than 2 down (10)
7 Each 2 and 6 down does its own .... (9) and, if senior management agrees, controls its own financial affairs.
9 The workers in a company must .... (7) customers' orders, or they may lose their jobs because the company may fail.
11 Workers do this to managers (6)

1
2
3
4 AFFAIRS
5
6
7
8
9
10
11
12
13

Becoming a manager

Complete the dialogue between the Managing Director (MD) and the Personnel Manager (PM). Choose from the words in the box. The first has been done for you.

sales	new technology
MBA	cost and price decisions
how to take decisions	manage
accounting for managers	promotion and marketing
communications	learn about management structures
distribution	read the balance sheet
specialised management-training courses	computer systems
results	

MD: John, we must think about (1) **specialised management-training courses** for our junior managers.

PM: Yes, our promising younger people need to (2) ....

MD: They need to know (3) ...., and the (4) .... of these decisions.

PM: And, of course, (5) .... is essential. And they must know how to (6) ....

MD: Without it, they will never (7) .... successfully, and they won't know anything about stock control, costing, pricing . . . you name it.

PM: Yes, (8) .... depend on knowing this.

MD: Of course, that's not the only thing they need to know. (9) .... means that they need to know about things like (10) ....

PM: What else?

MD: (11) ...., for example.

PM: Yes, and I think that the (12) .... departments need managers with this background, as well as the (13) .... department.

MD: Even the (14) .... managers could benefit, too.

MD: Perhaps we should only appoint managers with a Harvard (15) ....!

16 Business structure 1

Complete the organisation chart from the information provided. Two examples have been done for you. (Note that there are various ways of constructing an organisation chart. This is one of the most usual.)

The Managing Director (sometimes called the Chief Executive, or President in the USA) is the head of the company.

The company is run by a Board of Directors; each Director is in charge of a department. However, the Chairman of the Board is in overall control and may not be the head of any one department.

Most companies have Finance, Sales, Marketing (sometimes part of Sales), Production, Research and Development (R & D) and Personnel Departments. These are the most common departments, but some companies have others as well.

Most departments have a Manager, who is in charge of its day-to-day running, and who reports to the Director; the Director is responsible for strategic planning and for making decisions.

Various personnel in each department report to the Manager. One example, present in almost all companies, is the Sales Representative, who reports to the Sales Manager.

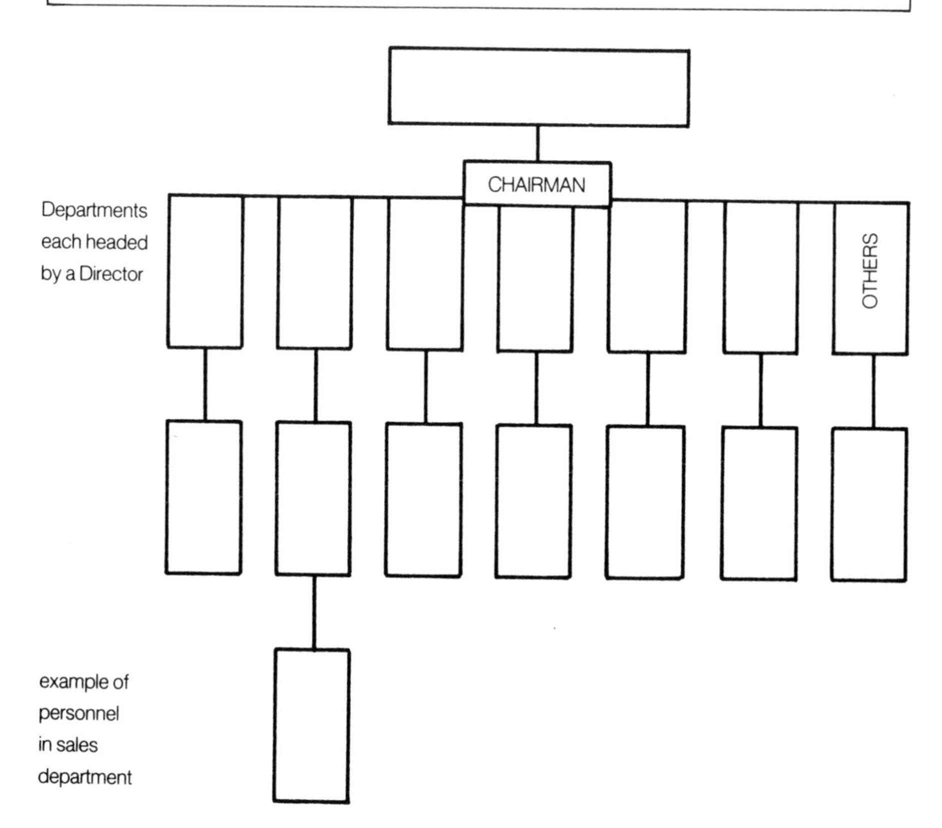

Business structure 2

Complete the sentences by choosing from the words below each sentence to fill in the gaps. The first has been done for you.

1 The employees responsible for carrying out general office duties, filling in forms and keeping statistics are ....a.... .

a clerks   b accountants   c supervisors

2 The employees who sell a company's products are the sales representatives, usually known as ....

a vendors   b renters   c reps

3 The employees who decide what to purchase, and who make the purchases of finished goods or components to be made into goods, are the ....

a choosers   b procurers   c buyers

4 The employees who are responsible for seeing that the finished goods are well made are the ....

a packers   b quality controllers   c financial staff

5 The clerical workers who use typewriters or word processors and who produce letters, memos or other documents, are ....

a secretaries   b editors   c copywriters

6 The employees who check a company's financial affairs are the ....

a statisticians   b accountants   c counters

7 The employees who are responsible for preparing checks, pay packets and payslips are the ....

a wages clerks   b filing clerks   c paying clerks

8 The workers who process data, under the control of managers and supervisors, are the computer ....

a hackers   b operators   c screeners

9 The person who greets a visitor and tells him or her how to get to the right office is the ....

a manager **b** president **c** receptionist

10 The employees who deal with a company's telephone calls are the ....

a VDU operators **b** telex operators
c switchboard operators

The branch office

Choosing from the words in the box, complete the passage by filling in the gaps. The first has been done for you.

branch office	hold stock	appointed
location	Head Office	safety
conditions	rent	transport
fire	premises	

Many companies open a (1) ...**branch**... ...**office**... to improve distribution in countries where a good market exists. The first step, of course, is to find suitable (2) .... in a good (3) ...., where the (4) .... is reasonable and (5) .... to retailers and distributors is fast and easy to arrange. Local (6) ...., including (7) .... precautions and (8) .... regulations, must be met; a manager must be (9) .... and staff must be found.

A decision must be made about whether the branch office is to (10) .... or not. The success or failure of this enterprise will depend on the relationship of the branch office to the (11) ...., and that must be established before any of the details are considered.

Making appointments

Fill in the missing words in the passages below. Choose from the following. The first has been done for you.

forms	employment	pay
personnel functions	promotion	holiday
references	round holes	square pegs
chosen	Applicants	Advertisements
short list	interview	

Making appointments is one of the main (1) **personnel functions** .
(2) .... are placed in newspapers and in trade journals. (3) .... who reply to these, or who are found in other ways, are sent application (4) .... From these the best candidates are (5) .... and a (6) .... is drawn up. The employers try to avoid fitting (7) .... into (8) .... The short-listed applicants are called for an (9) .... During this, the (10) .... package is explained; this includes the annual (11) .... entitlement, the rates of (12) ...., and the opportunities for (13) .... When the successful candidate is decided on, there is one last step: (14) .... are taken up before the appointment is finally confirmed.

Negotiating with trade unions

Read the passage and then read the clues and complete the crossword. All the words are in the passage and one word has been done for you.

Management must decide the overall strategy of a company, but must then join in negotiation with the workforce to resolve various issues or to agree compromises about them. Each point is discussed and each side guards its position; the Union will argue points which are important to its members. An offer may be made, which each side must refer – management to the Board, the Union to its members – to obtain the authority to accept it. If the negotiation reaches a deadlock, the Union may feel it has to call a strike. Only after this is settled can progress be made.

ACROSS

2 Unions and Management .... (4) in negotiation
4 Both sides .... (5) their case
5 Each side .... (6) the interests of the people it represents
6 Each item in a negotiation is a negotiating .... (5)
7 All-embracing planning for success: .... (8)
8 Points of discussion between the sides involved in a negotiation (6)
11 When each side agrees to give something up, a .... (10) is reached

DOWN

1 When agreement cannot be reached, a .... (8) has arisen
3 Noun made from a word in the title of this test .... (11)
4 For a successful negotiation, both sides must .... (5)
7 The last resort of the Unions, when negotiations fail .... (6)
9 A strike is said to be .... (7) when it is ended.
10 Each side has its own .... (8) in a negotiation
12 Management decides on an .... (5) to put to the Union
13 The Union must .... (5) Management's 12 down to its members.

1
2
3
4
5
6
7
8
9
10
11
12
13
COMPROMISE

Contracts

Fill in the gaps in the outline draft contract, choosing from the words in the box. The first has been done for you. (Note: "widget" is a slang term used for any type of imaginary item which is assumed to be made, bought or sold.)

terms	arbitration	payment
reclaim	freight/loading	specification
charges	penalty	late
delivery	substandard	invoked
letter of credit	parties	

DRAFT CONTRACT between
WIDGETRY Ltd (hereafter known as "the seller")
and MERCURY plc (hereafter known as "the buyer")

The seller undertakes to supply the buyer with 120,000 super widgets, to BSI (1) **specification** 999 and to pay all (2) .... and insurance (3) ....

The terms of (4) .... and immediate payment of (5) .... charges by confirmed and irrevocable (6) .... are to be standard.

A (7) .... clause will be included in the contract. It will be (8) .... against the seller for late delivery or (9) .... quality; against the buyer for (10) .... payment.

In the event of non-payment, the seller shall be entitled to (11) .... the goods.

In case of a dispute between the (12) .... to the contract, the matter will be taken to independent (13) .... All the (14) .... of the contract must be complied with by both parties.

Forecasts

Choose from the words in the box to complete the sentences. The first has been done for you.

net	market	loss	cash-flow	capital
sales	overheads	expenditure	gross	profit

1 The forecast which predicts how much money will be gained by a business is called the ....**profit**.... forecast.
2 The forecast which predicts how much money will be lost by a business is called the .... forecast.
3 The forecast which predicts how much money will be received or spent by a business is the .... forecast.
4 The forecast which predicts where most sales will be made, and what their value will be, is the .... forecast.
5 The forecast which predicts how much the company will sell is the .... forecast.
6 The forecast which predicts how much money will be spent by the company is the forecast of ....
7 The forecast which predicts how much money is needed to start up a business or to increase its wealth is the .... forecast.
8 The forecast which predicts how much money the company will earn before tax is paid is the .... profit forecast.
9 The forecast which predicts how much money the company will earn after tax is paid is the .... profit forecast.
10 The forecast which predicts how much money the company will have to spend on salaries, heating and lighting, rent, etc., is the forecast of ....

23 Agents and agencies

Mr Jones, Sales Director of a steel manufacturing company, is interviewing Mr Hollen, to see whether he would be a suitable agent to represent the company in a European country. Choosing from the words given, fill in the gaps, and complete the first part of the interview. The first has been done for you.

1 Jones: We thought we'd appoint a(n) ....**agent**.... to expand our business in Europe.

a agent **b** branch **c** department

2 Hollen: I expect you were thinking of a .... basis of, say, ten per cent, weren't you?

a discount **b** term **c** commission

3 Jones: Yes. And we'd send the goods on ....

a deposit **b** consignment **c** cover

4 Hollen: This would mean I could hold stocks, which would make it easier for me to develop new ....

a documents **b** markets **c** drafts

5 Jones: Yes, and we hope you could call on potential new ....

a sellers **b** bankers **c** customers

6 Hollen: They would be both .... and retailers, wouldn't they?

a wholesalers **b** stores **c** markets

7 And they might even become ....

a warehouses **b** stockists **c** stores

8 Jones: I'm sure you'd like this to be a .... agency, so that you know you needn't compete with others for our business?

a sole **b** unique **c** only

9 Hollen: Yes, please. And can you tell me what you have in mind about advertising and .... campaigns?

a after-sales **b** display **c** promotion

10 Jones: Well, we'd share the .... with you; we can negotiate the details after we've looked round the factory.

a costs **b** prices **c** terms

Takeovers and mergers

The definitions (in BLOCK CAPITAL LETTERS) in these sentences have got mixed up. Put them in the right place. The first has been done for you.

		Correct Word
1	When one company joins another to form a larger single company, the new company is the result of a BOTTOM LINE.	MERGER
2	When one company buys a majority of the shares of another, and so gains control, it has carried out a REDEPLOYMENT.	....
3	When the shares of this second company are bought quietly, without publicity, and usually in the shortest possible time, the first company has carried out a MANAGEMENT BUYOUT.	....
4	The REDUNDANCIES will try to negotiate good conditions for their members in the new company.	....
5	When a company is deciding whether to take over or to merge with another it will examine the accounts very carefully, paying particular attention to the EARLY RETIREMENT, which shows whether or not the company is profitable, and by how much.	....
6	Knowledge that a takeover is likely usually sends TRADE UNIONS up.	....
7	Sometimes, in an attempt to avoid a takeover, senior staff will attempt a DAWN RAID.	....
8	There are usually a number of SHARE PRICE after a merger or takeover.	....
9	As many staff as possible will undergo MERGER and be kept on in the new company.	....
10	Members of staff who do not wish to remain and work in the new company may take the option of TAKEOVER, perhaps with a reduced pension.	....

The protection of intellectual ownership

Choose the correct alternative to complete the sentences. The first has been done for you.

1 The protection of something so that it can be made or sold by one person only is by means of a ...**patent**... .

a patent **b** right **c** rule

2 The protection of books, plays, films, records etc is by means of a ....

a patent **b** microfiche **c** copyright

3 Most countries have laws to prevent the breaking of patent protection. Breaking these laws is ....

a piracy **b** burglary **c** felony

4 This protection, by patent or copyright, is the protection of the rights of ....

a property **b** ownership **c** justice

5 If employees discover or create something in the course of their work, the patent or copyright belongs to the ....

a employees **b** State **c** company

6 The right to manufacture copies of a protected work is given by a ....

a grant **b** licence **c** permit

7 Under some conditions, the protection in work can be ....

a waived **b** withdrawn **c** conceded

8 The period for which protection exists is the .... of the copyright or patent.

a term **b** length **c** date

9 The laws which prevent copying of protected material are the .... laws.

a licensing **b** conspiracy **c** antipiracy

10 Photocopying is a .... of copyright or patent protection.

a breach **b** contradiction **c** fraud

Targets and records

Choose from the words in the box to complete the sentences. The first one has been done for you.

sales	VAT	credit	growth	cash
production	creditors	stock	debtors	tax

1 A company plans how much money it wants to make in the coming year by setting a .....**sales**..... target.

2 To determine what a company actually has in its warehouse without physically counting the items, a company must keep .... records.

3 The Inland Revenue authorities need to see a company's .... records, usually once a year.

4 The .... target shows how many items a company intends to make in a given period of time.

5 HM Customs and Excise Department inspect a company's .... records, which have to be kept for six years.

6 The planned increase in sales and profits for next year over those for this year is the .... target.

7 A retailer's record of the cash – not the cheques or other forms of credit – that he receives and spends every day is shown by his .... sales records.

8 A retailer must also keep records of the sales which he makes but which are not paid for until later. These are shown in his .... sales records.

9 The names of people or firms to whom a company owes money are shown in its record of ....

10 The names of people or companies that owe money to the company are shown in the company's record of ....

The warehouse

Choose from the words in the box and write the numbers in the correct place. The first has been done for you.

1 shelving	**4** stock list	**7** labels	**10** forklift truck
2 packing area	**5** waste bin	**8** stencil	**11** orders
3 containers	**6** packing	**9** packers	**12** coffee machine

1
FRAGILE
TO

Money

Banking 1

The labels from the illustrations have got mixed up. Put them into the right place.

(1) **a** bank statement

(2) **b** cheque book

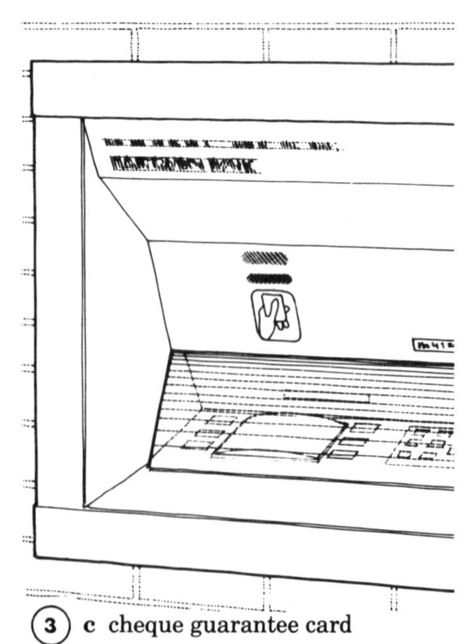

(3) **c** cheque guarantee card

(4) **d** Bureau de change

(5) **e** cash dispenser

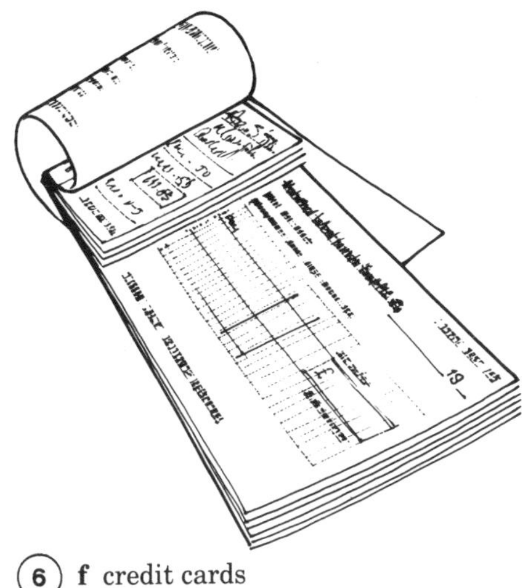

(6) **f** credit cards

(7) **g** charge cards

(8) **h** standing order

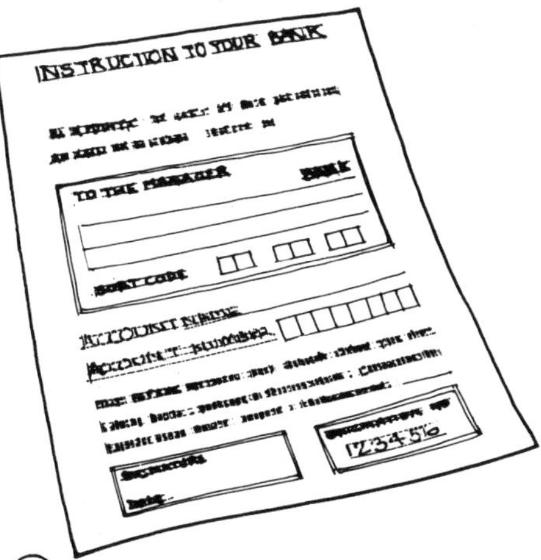

(9) **i** cashier

Banking 2

Choose from the words in the box to complete the sentences. The first has been done for you.

Bank of England	base rate	stock	shares	bond
bearer	Stock Exchange	bear	bull	asset

1. The American central bank, the FED, is the equivalent of the **Bank of England** in Britain.
2. The units of ownership of a company, allowing the holder to receive a proportion of the company's profits, are the ....
3. If the company is publicly quoted, the answer to 2 above are sold on the ....
4. In the UK, a fixed amount of paid-up capital held by a stockholder is a ....
5. If the market is thought to be good and prices on the Stock Exchange are thought to be likely to rise, the market is called a .... market.
6. If the market is thought to be poor and prices on the Stock Exchange are likely to fall, the market is called a .... market.
7. A promise to pay a sum of money over an agreed time by anyone licensed to do so, such as a government, insurance firm, etc., is a ....
8. Certificates of ownership of bonds that can be transferred from seller to buyer without any formalities are .... bonds.
9. Something that is owned by an individual or company, has monetary value, and can be sold to pay debts, is an ....
10. The interest which a bank charges on loans is at a rate which is usually higher than its ....

Rates, indexes and accounts

Choose from the words in the box to complete the sentences. The first has been done for you. (Note: the plural of *index* is, correctly, *indices*; however, *indexes* is in common use.)

VAT	close	bank	draw	FT
Dow Jones	Nikkei Dow	open	current	exchange
interest				

RATES

1 The sum borrowers pay to lenders for the use of their money is determined by the **interest** rate.

2 The value of the money of one country compared to that of another is shown by the .... rate.

3 The rate of the tax added to the price of an article, paid by the buyer to the seller, and by the seller to the government is the .... rate.

4 The rate of interest fixed by a central bank, such as the Bank of England, is the .... rate.

INDEXES

5 The index of share prices in America is the .... index.

6 The index of share prices in Britain is the .... index.

7 The index of share prices in Japan is the .... index.

ACCOUNTS

8 The bank account that covers daily needs – salaries are paid into it, cash is drawn from it, and cheques are written against it – is the .... account.

9 To start an account with a bank or with a supplier is to .... it; to finish using an account with a bank or with a supplier and formally to end the arrangement is to .... it.

10 To obtain cash from a bank at which one has an account is to .... out cash.

Accounts 1

The letters in the words on the right are in the wrong order. Rearrange them and put the word, with the letters in the correct order, into the gaps in the sentences. The first has been done for you and the first letter of each word is given.

1 Items which the business expects to keep for a year or more are its f **ixed** assets. *xidfe*

2 Money used to operate a business on a day-to-day basis is its w .... capital. *girwokn*

3 The account which describes the trading activities of a business over a (stated) period of time is the p .... and loss account. *tforpi*

4 A statement produced, usually at the end of a financial year, showing the financial state of the business and including, among other things, its assets and liabilities, is its b .... sheet. *nablaec*

5 When one company attempts to gain control of another, by buying a majority of its shares, it is making a t .... bid. *eotkrvea*

6 The ledger containing creditors' accounts is the b .... ledger. *thubog*

7 To enter an item in a ledger is to p .... it to that ledger. *stop*

8 Ledgers are written up from entries in day b .... *sokob*

9 A note which accompanies goods sent by a seller, to be signed by the person who receives the goods, is a d .... note. *riveleyd*

10 A document showing what has been bought and for how much, and indicating that the goods are in transit, is an a .... note. *vaiecd*

Accounts 2

Fill in the missing first and last letters in the words below. A clue is given for each word.

	Word	Clue
1	_ P P L I C A T I O _	The first/second/third time a debtor is written to and asked for payment, a letter of .... is sent.
2	_ T A T U _	An enquiry to a bank, asking whether a customer is credit-worthy, is a .... enquiry.
3	_ E T T L E M E N _	Payment of a debt in cash is a cash ....
4	_ R E D I _	The greatest sum which debtors are allowed to owe is their .... limit.
5	_ E B I _	Items for which payment is owed appear on an account as .... items.
6	_ O T _	Items to be paid to a creditor are shown on a credit ....
7	_ I S C O U N _	A percentage deduction made for an order over a stated value, or payment within a stated time, is a ....
8	_ R O ■ F O R M _	A document issued as a temporary statement, to be replaced by a final invoice at a later date, is a .... invoice.
9	_ A I S _	To draw up an invoice is to .... it.
10	_ A L A N C _	The complete statement, showing what is owed or possessed, provides a statement of the .... of the account.

33 Accounts 3

What do the abbreviations stand for? The first one has been done for you.

1 C/N **credit note**

2 D/N ....

3 A/C ....

4 L/C ....

5 B/L ....

6 c.i.f. ....

7 f.o.b. ....

8 c. and f. ....

9 D/A ....

10 D/P ....

Accounts 4

Match the definitions to the words in the box. The first has been done for you.

remuneration	expenses	salary
return	adjust	numbered
account rendered	profit (margin)	credit terms
wages		

1 Fixed regular pay each month for a job, especially a job done by a senior member of staff ......**salary**......

2 Payment for labour or services, usually paid every day or every week, and often based on the number of hours worked ....

3 Payment for work done or trouble taken; a reward ....

4 To change slightly, especially to correct a mistake or to adapt to new conditions, including financial changes ....

5 In order for people or institutions to provide money, especially for companies, they must see a good chance of making money by getting a good rate of this ....

6 In a ledger, every account is this ....

7 The difference between the cost and the selling price ....

8 A member of staff who has spent money on company business is reimbursed after making this claim ....

9 A reference to a bill which has been sent but not yet paid ....

10 A statement of how much discount is available, and for what. It appears on an invoice ....

Insurance

The words on the right have their letters in the wrong order. Rearrange the letters so that they are in the correct order. The first has been done for you, and the first letter of each word is given.

1 The details of an agreement with an insurance company shown in a written insurance p olicy . *lyopci*

2 Insurance arrangements are made through b .... *ksborre*

3 Professionals, like those in 2, are usually able to obtain the best insurance r .... *saert*

4 An all r .... policy specifies the hazards that are covered by that policy. *isksr*

5 A loss by one shipper, but which is shared by all the shippers with cargoes on the same carrying vessel, is the general a .... *gaevrae*

6 A partial loss of a consignment, which may not affect other consignments on the same carrying vessel, is a p .... average. *auipratclr*

7 A policy with a s .... risks clause covers the goods against theft, short delivery, breakage and leakage, other forms of damage and so on. *liapsec*

8 Regular shippers may often take out a f .... insurance policy, which gives automatic cover for a fixed value of shipments, depending on the previous year's values, if the insurance company is told when each shipment is made. *ilatfogn*

9 A flexible type of insurance, for twelve months and at agreed rates, is o .... cover. *poen*

10 Ships' cargoes are covered by m .... policies. *rmenai*

36 Finance 1

Fill in the missing word(s) in each of the following sentences. Choose from the alternatives beneath each sentence. The first has been done for you.

1 The Board of **Directors** is responsible for deciding on and controlling the strategy of a corporation or company.

a Workers **b** Directors **c** Control

2 Small businesses depend on investors providing .... capital.

a venture **b** individual **c** cooperative

3 Investors are influenced by the projected .... on their capital.

a market **b** return **c** rate

4 The capital needed to run a business is provided by ....

a gain **b** risk **c** investment

5 Rent and rates, which do not change as turnover volume changes, make up the .... costs of a company.

a fixed **b** contribution **c** variable

6 Materials and direct labour costs, which change as turnover volume changes, make up the .... costs of a company.

a fixed **b** contribution **c** variable

7 Every company must watch its .... carefully if it is to avoid bankruptcy.

a market managers **b** cash flow **c** production lines

8 The .... account shows whether the company is profitable or not.

a profit and loss **b** volume **c** shareholders

9 Banks require .... to guarantee a loan.

a accounts **b** shares **c** securities

10 Insurance companies may use .... to negotiate the amount of insurance to be paid.

a claim forms **b** tariff companies **c** insurance adjusters

11 The Stock Exchange deals with the purchase and sale of ....

a stocks and shares **b** bulls and bears **c** statements and invoices

12 An individual or a company buying a block of shares in another company to give itself a majority shareholding is making a ....

a management buyout **b** takeover bid **c** dawn raid

37 Finance 2

PART A

Choose from the words in the box to complete the definitions. The first has been done for you.

bookkeeping	interest	creditor	company
profit	current	capital	net
shares	debtor	dividend	statement

1 Recording financial transactions is **bookkeeping** .

2 A legal organisation, formally registered in one of three ways, and having a life independent of its members, is a ....

3 A person or organisation that owes money is a ....

4 A person or organisation to whom money is owed is a ....

5 The assets, including cash, debtors and stocks used in a company's trading, available at the present moment, are its .... assets.

6 The equal parts into which the ownership of a company is divided are its ....

7 The money paid to shareholders out of a company's profits is the ....

8 A company's turnover, less its cost of sales, is its gross ....

9 A company's turnover after the cost of sales, tax, rent and other liabilities are deducted is its .... profit.

10 The sum of money paid by a borrower to a lender for the use of the lender's money is the .... on the loan.

11 The document sent to the debtor by the creditor, showing how much is owed and for what, is the .... of account.

12 The shareholders' investment in a company is the share ....

PART B

Now find the words in the word square. The words may read from left to right, from right to left, from top to bottom, from bottom to top, or diagonally. One example has been done to help you.

B	U	T	S	E	R	E	T	N	I	X	A	Y
P	O	B	Q	C	A	L	T	R	E	N	U	O
C	M	O	H	K	R	C	A	P	I	T	A	L
O	C	A	K	L	D	E	B	T	O	R	I	T
M	S	Y	W	K	D	L	F	E	N	P	D	U
P	C	U	R	R	E	N	T	P	A	B	I	L
A	C	S	H	A	R	E	S	Y	M	O	V	A
N	D	E	Z	L	N	X	P	R	O	F	I	T
Y	P	T	E	Q	T	R	L	I	Y	Z	D	P
R	O	T	I	D	E	R	C	X	N	T	E	H
E	L	S	W	A	D	E	R	T	L	G	N	S
S	T	A	T	E	M	E	N	T	E	A	D	F

Audits – the year-end nightmare

Fill in the gaps to complete the passage, choosing from the words in the box. The first one has been done for you.

accounts	stocks	reconcile
books	write down	invoices
receipts	depreciate	auditors
public	Companies	Exchange
firms	VAT	annual

An official examination, the audit, is made of the (1) ..**accounts**.. of a business; this is usually done once each year. Independent (2) .... descend on a company and examine all the company's accounts for the previous year; this is known, colloquially, as "checking the (3) .... ".

The auditors attempt to (4) .... all the bank statements, checking them against the (5) .... and (6) .... They check all the company's (7) .... ; if the value of any of them has decreased during the year, they (8) ....its value to a realistic one – many items (9) .... with time and use. Although (10) .... returns have to be submitted to the Customs and Excise authorities every three months, they are checked again during the audit.

A (11) .... company – one of which the shares are quoted on the Stock (12) .... – must lodge its accounts in (13) .... House, where they are available to the public, and to possible investors.

The (14) .... audit is a legal requirement in Britain; many professional (15) .... of accountants only do this work and do not need to undertake any other type of work.

Selling

The sales department

Unfortunately the notes of an important meeting were accidentally destroyed. The Sales Manager's Secretary managed to retrieve some of them, but some words were missing. She and the Sales Manager remembered most of what had been said at the meeting. Choosing from the box, fill in the missing words. The first has been done for you.

Director	promotion	appoint	credit-worthy	forms
territory	open	reps	agent	fax

The Sales (1) **Director** had to go to a Board meeting, so the new manager saw the (2) .... instead. The agent said that the (3) .... did not visit his customers often enough, so his campaign for the (4) .... of the new line had to be changed, and it was difficult to cover the (5) .... properly. He wanted the authority to (6) .... a rep to cover the northern part of his area. If he could get this help, he could find new customers, (7) .... new accounts if the customers were (8) ...., and service or close existing accounts. He also wanted to replace his telex machine by a (9) .... machine, because it would be much better for reproducing order (10) ...., so that he and the warehouse could see exactly what was needed and could also get the information much more quickly.

40 Retailing 1

Write the numbers of the words in the correct place. One has been done for you.

1 cash till	**5** customers	**9** delivery van
2 counter	**6** counter staff	**10** car park
3 cashier	**7** office staff	**11** packers
4 safe	**8** manager	**12** Mail-Order Department

1

Retailing 2

The words in the box have their letters in the wrong order. Choose from them to complete the sentences below and write the word, with the letters in the correct order, in the gaps below. The first has been done for you, and the first letter of each word is given.

sols raeled	nidedmaml	wrlahesole
rutrnoev	utsciond	kocts tnloocr
icysretu	hsovadeer	hacs dna cryra
aihnc		

1. A **loss** **leader** is something sold very cheaply to encourage customers to come into a shop; once they are in, they may buy other things at profitable prices.
2. The amount of money taken (without any deductions) or the amount of goods sold, is the t ....
3. Deciding how many items should be ordered, and when, is a matter of s .... c ....
4. A number of shops belonging to one company is a c ....
5. Shops possess safes for s ....
6. A retailer buys his goods at a d .... and sells them at a retail price to produce a profit.
7. A retailer buys his stock from a w ....
8. The costs of running a retail operation caused by lighting, heating, rent, wages, etc., are its o ....
9. The retailer is the m .... between the manufacturer or wholesaler and the customer.
10. The everyday name for a warehouse from which a retailer collects the goods himself or herself is a c .... a .... c ....

Marketing and promotion

Choose the correct word from the box to complete the passage. The first one has been done for you.

Advertisements	exhibitions	Trade
copy-writer	set up	Commerce
promotion	market	price sensitivity
copy	Marketing	controls
designer	media	budgets
trade magazines		

(1) **Marketing** and (2) .... involve letting potential customers know about a new product both before it is made and after it becomes available for sale. (3) .... in the local and national press and (4) .... in areas where there is likely to be a good market are among the ways in which this is done; the choice of (5) .... – magazines, newspapers, radio and TV – for the advertisements and of locations for exhibitions is made as a result of thorough (6) .... research, so that money (all marketing departments have tightly controlled (7)) .... is spent where it is most likely to produce results. The advertising (8) ...., usually provided by a specialist (9) .... and set out by a (10) .... to have the most impact, is probably the most common form of promotion, although the way in which stands are (11) .... at exhibitions is also extremely important. "News" items leaked to (12) .... are also important – and they are free! (13) .... Associations and Chambers of (14) .... can provide advice about the size of markets, their location, and also about such things as (15) .... and import (16) .... in specific areas.

Complaints 1: Making a complaint

The labels from the illustrations have got mixed up. Put them into the right place.

a I'll never come here again!

b I'm afraid I don't see what we can do about this.

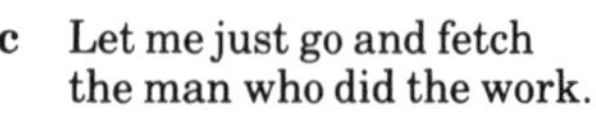
c Let me just go and fetch the man who did the work.

d But this is the part that really matters; unless you can put this right, I can't use the machine.

e There are a lot of things wrong with this and I need them all put right.

f This is John, who actually did the work.

g I'm the manager. What seems to be the problem?

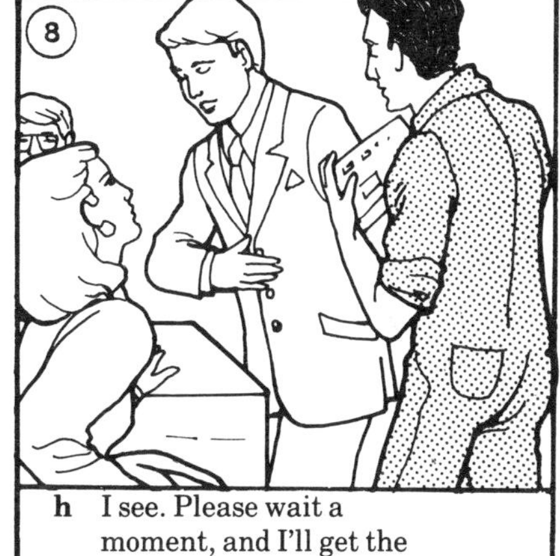

h I see. Please wait a moment, and I'll get the manager.

i I want to make a complaint. Can I talk to someone about it, please?

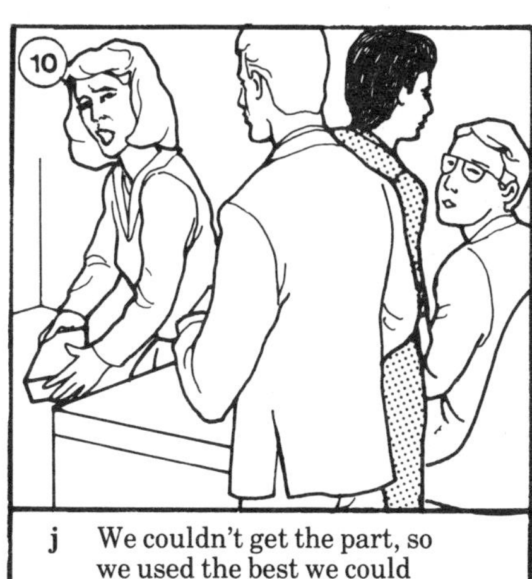

j We couldn't get the part, so we used the best we could get. We thought it would work.

Complaints 2: The reply

"The customer is always right."

The text of a letter replying to a complaint is given. Complete it, choosing from the alternatives given to fill in the gaps. The first has been done for you.

1	**a**	the 25 of October	**b**	October the 25	**c**	25th October
2	**a**	defect	**b**	problem	**c**	asset
3	**a**	demand	**b**	order	**c**	request
4	**a**	investigated	**b**	looked	**c**	traced
5	**a**	bothered	**b**	killed	**c**	horrified
6	**a**	suppliers	**b**	creators	**c**	models
7	**a**	mislabelled	**b**	misspelt	**c**	mishandled
8	**a**	certified	**b**	checked	**c**	tried
9	**a**	apologise	**b**	sorry	**c**	regret
10	**a**	suggest	**b**	demand	**c**	insist
11	**a**	charge	**b**	subtract	**c**	reimburse
12	**a**	debit	**b**	cost	**c**	credit

Thank you for your letter of (1) ....c.... 1989, about the (2) .... you have had with your (3) .... X/123/89.

I have (4) .... into the matter and I was (5) .... to find that our (6) .... had sent us the wrong components and had also (7) .... them, so that our clerks did not realise the mistake. Of course we should have (8) ...., but I am (9) .... to say that we did not do so.

The only thing I can do is to (10) .... that you return the faulty items (we will, of course, (11) .... the shipping costs) and we will replace them with the correct items or (12) .... you with their value.

We apologise for the error and are taking steps to ensure that it is not repeated.

Orders

Choose from the words in the box, and put the word into the correct place. One has been done for you.

order no.	Your ref./Our ref.	Quantity	Total cost
Catalogue/item no.	Packing	Discounts	subtotal
Authorised signature	Description	Delivery address	Unit cost
Date	Marks		

COLISEUM MOTORS
1, rue des Bagndes 75023 Paris, France

To Camford Spares Ltd
Oxbridge House
Bletchley
Avon XL82 95AG
England

Purchase (1) **order no** ....

(2) ....: 6th March 19––

(3) CM/JS/76
.... CS/L/S/87

Please supply the following

(4)	(5)	(6)	(7)	(8) ....
5	931A	fan motor assembly	£199.99	£999.95
100	1052C	brake pipes	£45.00	£4,500.00
20	52K	steering dampers	£50.00	£1,000.00
10	531P	radiators	£95.00	£950.00
25	193T	front fog lights	£6.50	£162.50
			(9)	£7,612.45
		Less (13)		
		5% for orders over £1,000	£380.62	
		2½% for settlement within 30 days	£190.31	£570.93
			TOTAL	£7,041.52

Date required:
1 June 19––

(10) ....
5 cartons

(11) .... CMX 1 – 5

(12) ....

(14) ....

Coliseum Motors
1, rue des Bagndes
75023 Paris
France

Foreign trade

Import/export 1: Abbreviations

Which abbreviation fits the definition? Choose from the box. The first has been done for you.

EC	c.i.f.	D/P	L/C	D/A
B/L	B/E	c. and f.	f.o.b.	sp.ex.

1 The formal union of some European countries under the Treaty of Rome. **EC**

2 A document by which a buyer undertakes to pay a seller through a bank if the seller delivers the goods according to the terms of the contract. It can be documentary or irrevocable. ....

3 A document signed by a ship's Master to say that he has received the cargo, to which it acts as title. ....

4 A contract in which the seller agrees to pay for the transport of the goods to their destination and for insuring them on the journey. ....

5 A contract in which the seller pays for the delivery of the goods to a given destination. ....

6 An order to pay for goods. It is drawn by an exporter and requires payment by the buyer, who must accept it formally by signing his name. ....

7 The documents are supplied only when the money is paid. ....

8 The documents are supplied when the bill of exchange is accepted. ....

9 A special price for goods sold overseas, usually less than for goods sold at home. ....

10 A contract in which the seller pays all charges up to and including the loading of goods on to the train ship or which will deliver them to the buyer. ....

Import/export 2

Complete the words in the boxes. The first one has been done for you.

1. Goods under the control of the Customs and Excise authorities are [B][O][N][D][E][D] goods.
2. A draft payable on presentation is a [S][ ][ ][ ][T] draft.
3. An invoice which is certified, in the exporting country, by the consulate of the country of destination is a [ ][ ][ ][ ][U][L][ ][ ] invoice.
4. The original copy of a B/E of exchange is known as the [ ][ ][R][ ][T] of [ ][X][C][ ][ ][ ][ ][E]
5. The charge made for carrying goods from one country to another is the [ ][R][ ][ ][G][H][ ] charge.
6. Selling goods outside the seller's country is [ ][X][P][ ][ ][T][ ][ ][G] them.
7. Buying goods from another country is [ ][M][P][ ][ ][T][ ][ ][G] them.
8. Goods sent to be sold by an agent at the highest possible price are sent on [C][ ][ ][S][ ][G][N][ ][ ][ ][ ]
9. If no duties are charged on imported or exported goods, they are duty- [ ][ ][E][ ]
10. If goods are damaged or lost, their value will be reimbursed by an [I][ ][ ][U][ ][ ][ ][ ][E] company.

Import/export 3

Complete the following passage by choosing from the words in the box to fill in the gaps. The first has been done for you.

imports	market research	agents	customs
exporting	commission	invoices	certificates
profit margin	stock(s)	foreign	export

Importing and (1) **exporting** are the two aspects of foreign trade: a country spends money on goods it (2) .... and gains money through its exports. Valuable though (3) .... trade is for keeping domestic prices down by creating competition at home and providing large markets abroad, governments may have to put restrictions on it, which they usually do by subjecting imports to (4) .... duties or by restricting some types of exports.

Customs authorities must make sure that imported goods are not sold at a lower price than that in their country of origin; to assess the domestic price they require consular (5) .... or (6) .... of value and origin.

Large firms may have their own import and (7) .... departments, but both large and small firms deal with clearing and forwarding (8) .... who handle all the details of transporting cargo.

When goods are sold abroad, buyers who are stockists will have to pay for (9) .... for which they will not receive payment for some time; they must, therefore, work on a higher (10) .... to cover this. Many buyers prefer to become foreign agents who work on (11) ....; they will not then have to pay for the goods but they must obtain the highest possible prices when the goods are sold.

So, after careful (12) ...., a manufacturer can sell to a large export market if he has the right products, of the right quality, and sells them at the right price.

Shipping 1

Choose from the words in the box to complete the passage. The first has been done for you.

cargo	forwarding	shipping
documents	Excise	manifest
services	destination	cleared
consignments		

The (1) ....**cargo**..... carried by a ship is listed in the (2) ...., which is a list of the bills of lading covering all the (3) .... on that vessel for that voyage. It is just one of the (4) .... that are involved in the shipping of goods; the insurance policy and commercial invoice are among the others. The Customs and (5) .... authorities will examine all these.

Clearing and (6) .... agents are often used to handle the transportation of goods. They will arrange for the loading and unloading of the goods and arrange all the dock (7) .... that are needed.

The (8) .... marks, which are stencilled on the cases, provide an easy way of identifying the items in a consignment when they are unloaded. The marks are described in the manifest, which is again inspected when the goods are (9) .... through Customs on reaching their (10) ....

Shipping 2

Below is part of a telephone conversation between a manufacturer, Mr Jones, and a clearing and forwarding agent, Mr Brown. Choose from the words in the box to complete the conversation. The first has been done for you.

documentation	ex works	customs
declaration	present	transport
licence	stencilled	bill of lading
pro forma		

Jones: . . . So you feel that the (1) **documentation** isn't complete yet?
Brown: No, I'm afraid not. I'm not at all sure what (2) .... has been arranged to get the goods to Southampton.
Jones: I'll ask our shipper – we're using Carson and Napier this time – and I'll get them to let you know.
Brown: Please make sure that we get a list of the marks (3) .... on the container.
Jones: Yes, I'll do that. And we have the export (4) ...., which we'll send on to you. We've made the (5) .... at the consulate, so we're getting the consular invoices which will confirm the (6) .... cost of the consignment. Will you send it through to the importing (7) .... authorities, or shall we?
Brown: We'll do that for you. Have you sent a copy, with the other documents, to your bank so that they can (8) .... them all through the Bank of South America?
Jones: Not yet, because there's been a delay with the (9) .... For some reason they've put the wrong number of packages on it, so we're just waiting for that to be cleared up. We'll get it off as soon as we can.
Brown: Good. And there should be no trouble with the terms since they've already seen a (10) .... invoice.
Jones: No, there was no problem at all.

Answers

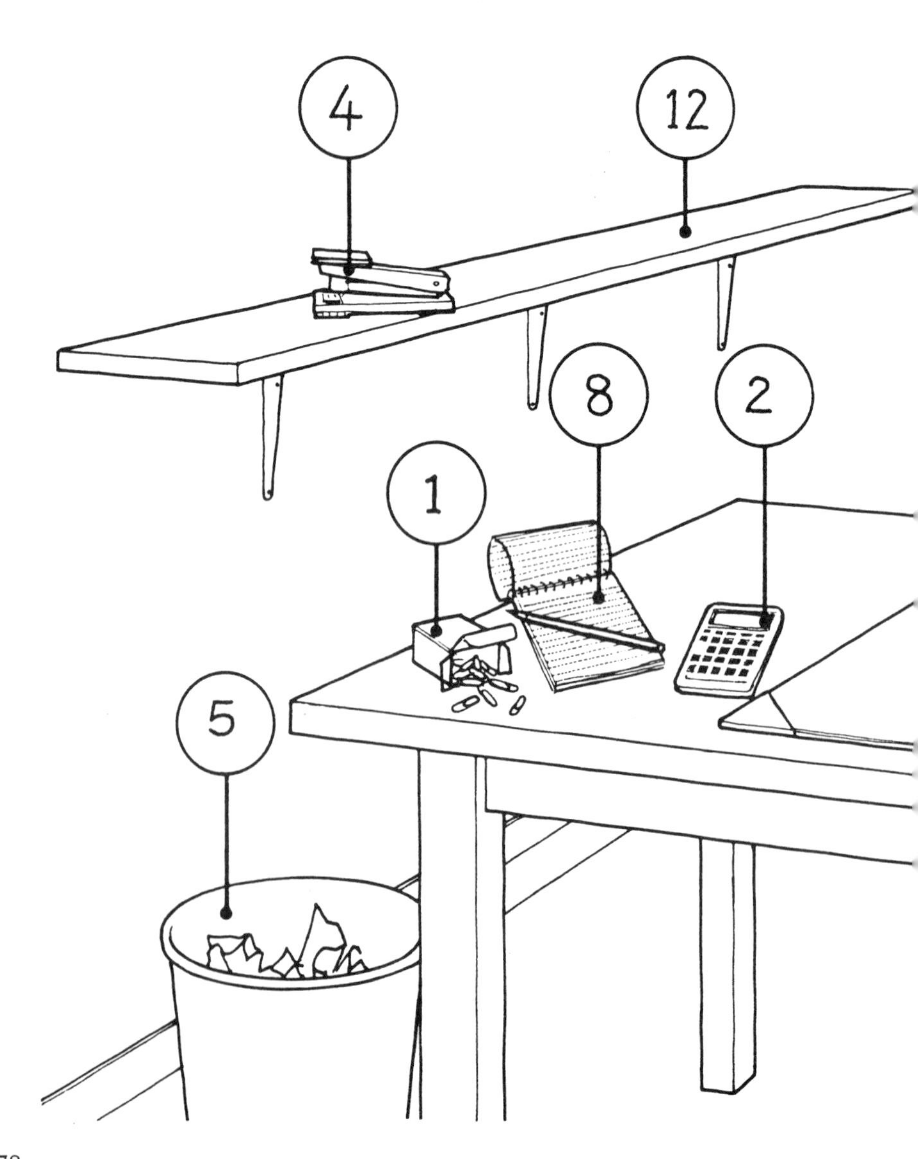
4
12
8
2
1
5

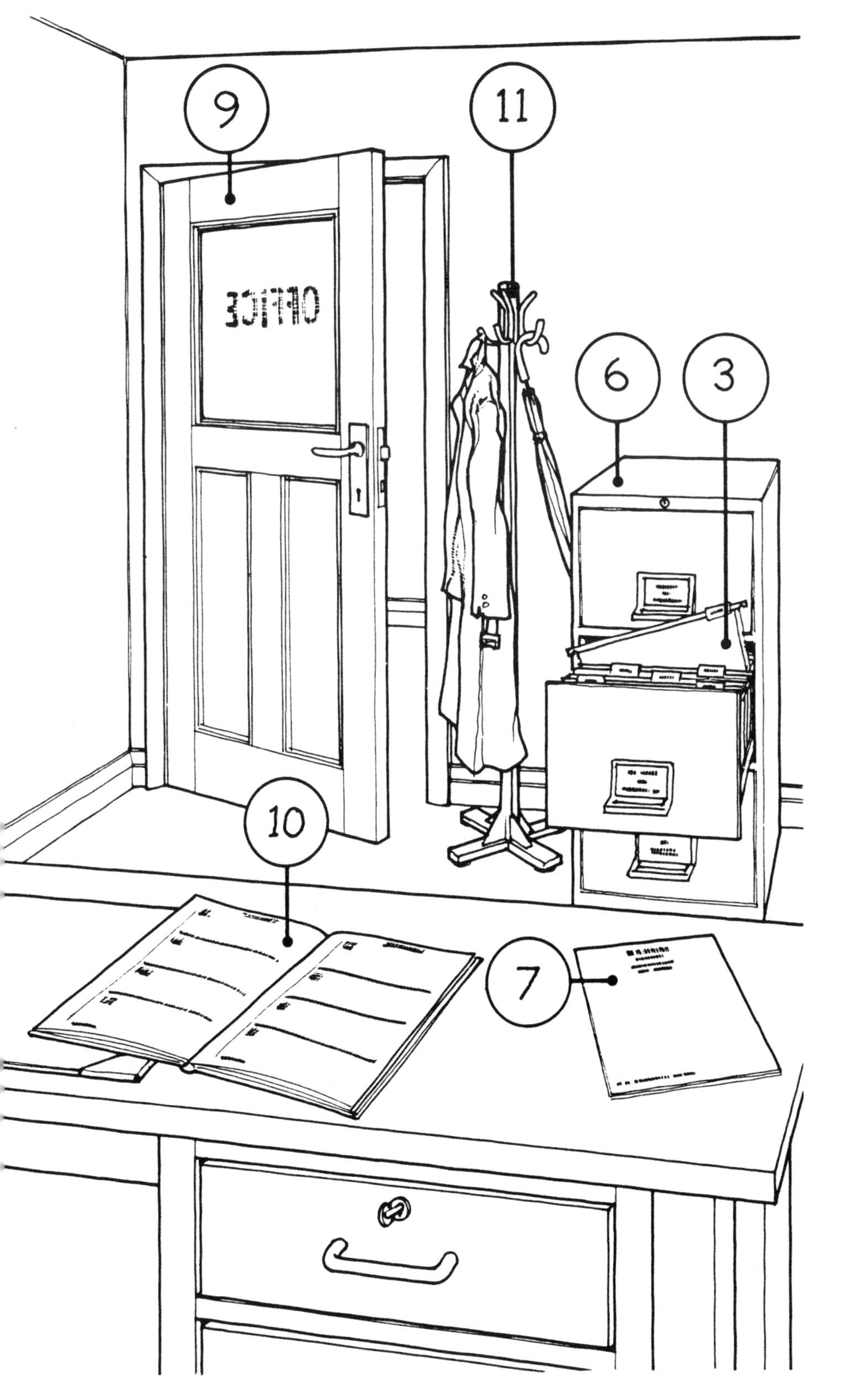
9
11
OFFICE
6
3
10
7

TEST 2

1 shorthand
2 typing
3 typewriter
4 word processor
5 audio typing
6 notebook
7 diary
8 letters
9 memos
10 minutes
11 petty cash
12 post book
13 screen
14 proof reading

TEST 3

1 travel arrangements
2 travel agents
3 international telephone operator
4 directory enquiries
5 previous correspondence
6 circulation
7 system
8 index
9 reference
10 job
11 personal assistant
12 responsibility

TEST 4

1 dictation
2 shorthand
3 w.p.m.
4 training
5 diary
6 post book
7 petty cash
8 confidential secretary
9 franking machine
10 word processor

TEST 5

1 twelve thousand four hundred and two
2 one million one thousand one hundred and eleven
3 twenty-one
4 point one five
5 point nought nought two/zero two hundredths
6 one quarter/a quarter
7 one half/a half
8 one third/a third
9 1,754,321
10 1,000,000,000
11 92
12 3,402
13 199.99999... or 199.9
14 ·02
15 1·8
16 (12 × 8 =) 72
17 (38 × 2 =) 76
18 (144 ÷ 12 =) 12
19 (8 × 50,000 =) 400,000
20 (3 × 1,500,000 =) 4,500,000

TEST 6

1 T
2 T
3 T
4 F (this service has been discontinued)
5 F
6 T
7 F (most countries charge less for calls made outside business hours)
8 T
9 T
10 F (the code for a city is usually changed if it follows the code for a country)
11 F
12 T
13 F (it is the State in the US which is roughly the equivalent of a county in Britain)
14 T

TEST 7

1 a – check-in desk
2 g – flight number
3 k – departure time
4 d – boarding pass
5 h – ticket
6 l – departure lounge
7 b – reception desk
8 c – twin-bedded double room
9 f – double room
10 e – single room
11 i – private bath
12 j – check-out time

TEST 8

1 letterhead
2 (sender's) address
3 recipient's address
4 references
5 date
6 salutation
7 introductory paragraph
8 main paragraph
9 concluding paragraph
10 complimentary ending
11 signature
12 (typed) signature
13 position/title
14 enclosures

TEST 9

The correct order is: 2 3 7 5 10 12 9 11 4 6 1 8

TEST 10

1 Present
2 Apologies
3 Minutes of the last meeting
4 Seconder
5 subcommittee
6 Members
7 chairman
8 Proposer
9 chaired
10 Action
11 Any Other Business
12 Date of next meeting

TEST 11 See pages 82–3

TEST 12

Part A

1 bugs
2 chips
3 information; processing
4 graphics
5 ROM (Read Only Memory)
6 RAM (Random Access Memory)
7 load
8 systems
9 WYSIWYG (This is pronounced 'wisi-wig'. It means that what you see on the screen represents almost exactly what will appear on paper when it is printed out.)
10 files
11 controls
12 scroll

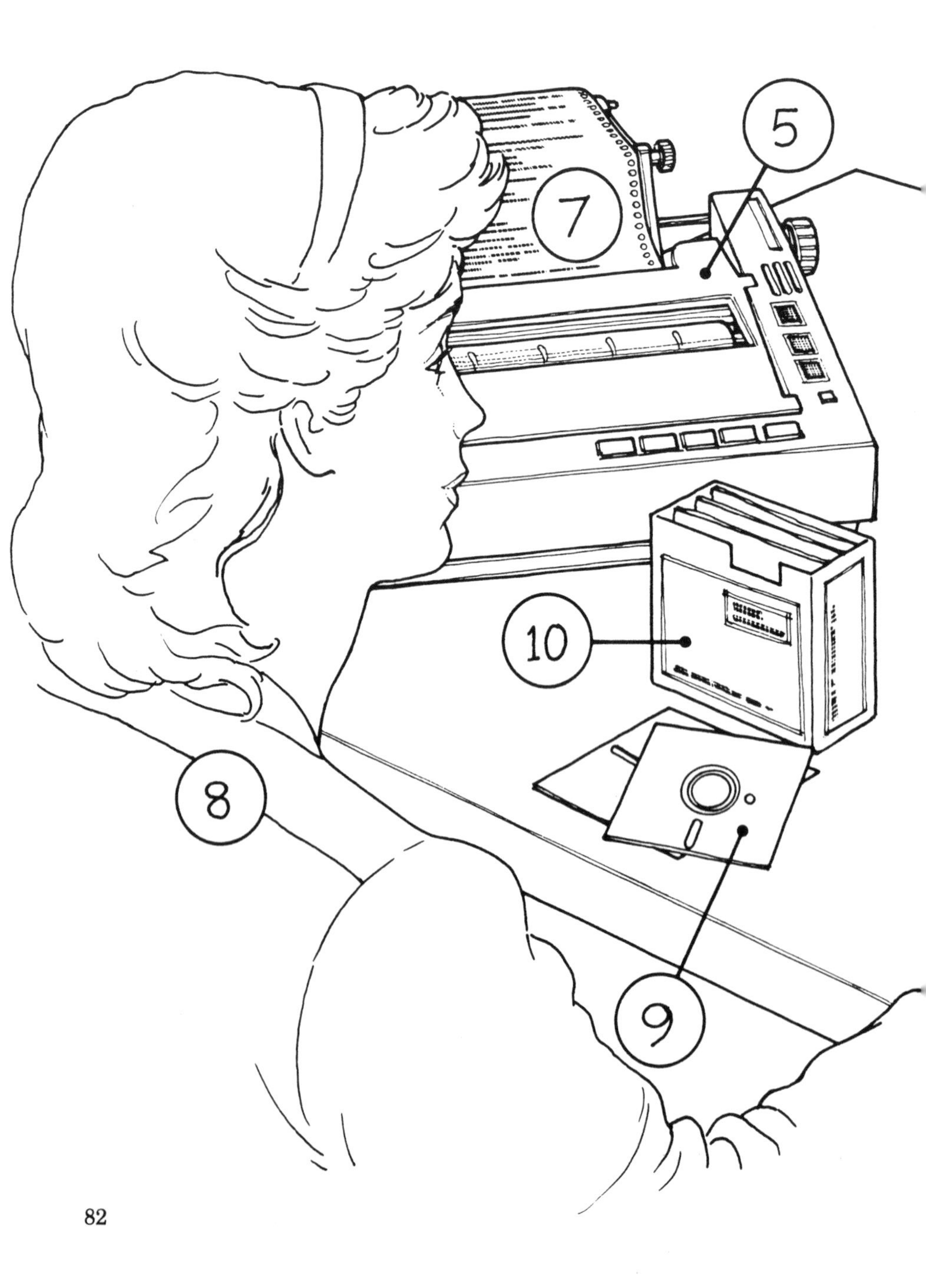
5
7
10
8
9

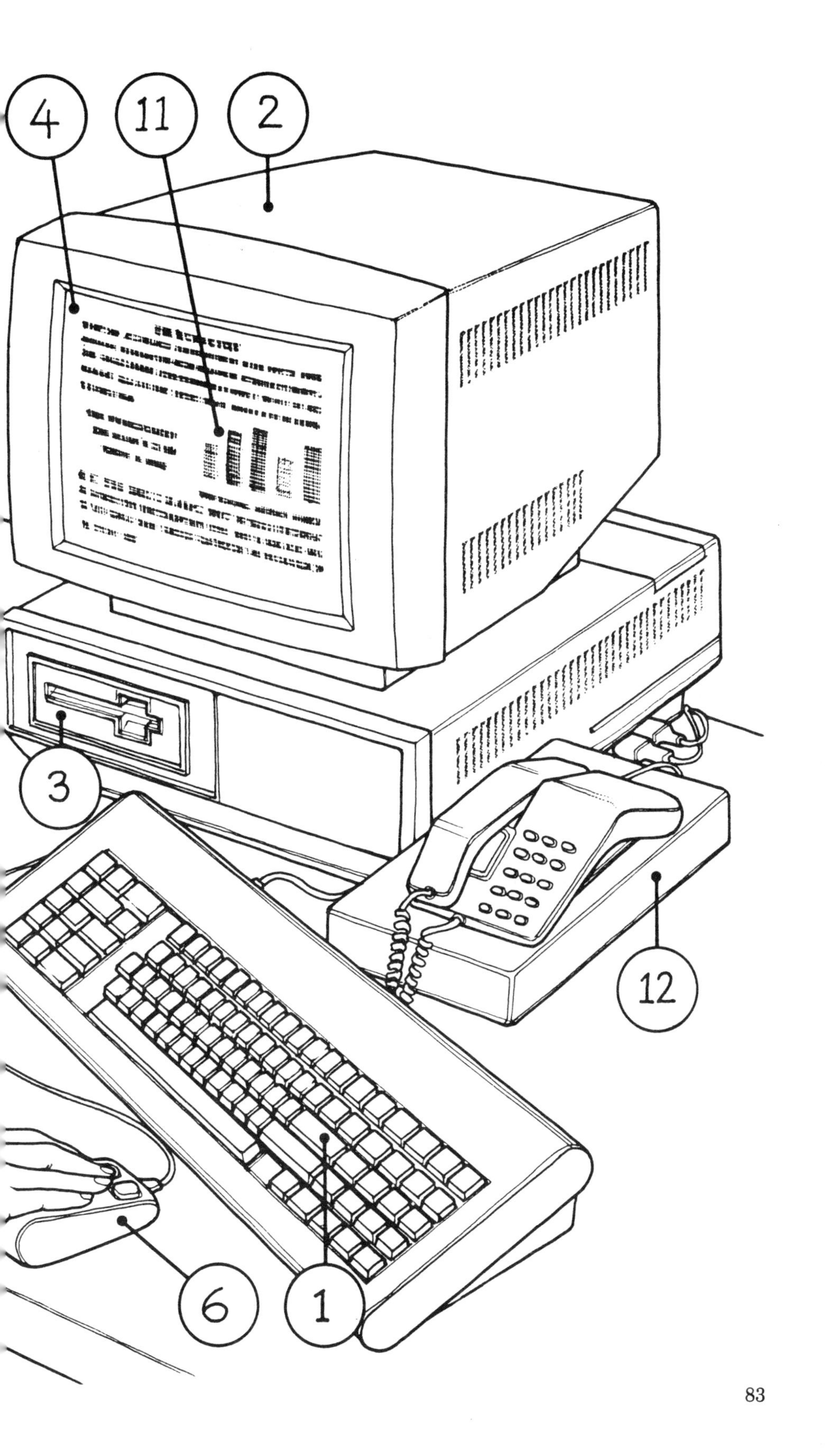
4
11
2
3
12
6
1

TEST 12 Part B

P	C	H	I	P	S	E	F	U	L	P
R	O	O	P	R	Z	I	I	H	D	N
O	N	K	U	O	F	T	L	R	A	O
C	T	Y	R	O	M	S	E	R	P	I
E	R	W	F	E	Q	I	S	O	L	T
S	O	N	S	Y	S	T	E	N	S	A
S	L	W	Y	S	I	W	Y	G	T	M
I	S	P	L	I	C	D	B	R	A	R
N	L	A	E	T	N	O	M	A	H	O
G	L	P	R	G	T	U	E	P	V	F
N	O	M	B	I	D	N	T	H	S	N
X	R	A	U	L	A	M	L	I	S	I
Y	C	R	G	R	O	I	P	C	N	A
Z	S	L	S	U	L	P	U	S	T	X

TEST 13

1 hardware
2 software
3 programs
4 word processing
5 spreadsheets
6 database management programs
7 accounting programs
8 graphics
9 communications programs
10 desktop publishing programs
11 keys in/types in
12 saved
13 retrieved
14 personal computers
15 network
16 mainframe computer
17 IBM compatible

TEST 14

Across
1 Price
3 Unit
4 Affairs
5 Cost
8 Delegation
10 Ex
12 Stop
13 Target

Down
1 Profitable
2 Division
6 Department
7 Budgeting
9 Execute
11 Report

TEST 15

1 specialised management-training courses
2 learn about management structures
3 how to take decisions
4 results
5 accounting for managers
6 read the balance sheet
7 manage
8 cost and price decisions
9 new technology
10 computer systems
11 communications
12 promotion and marketing
13 sales
14 distribution
15 MBA

TEST 16

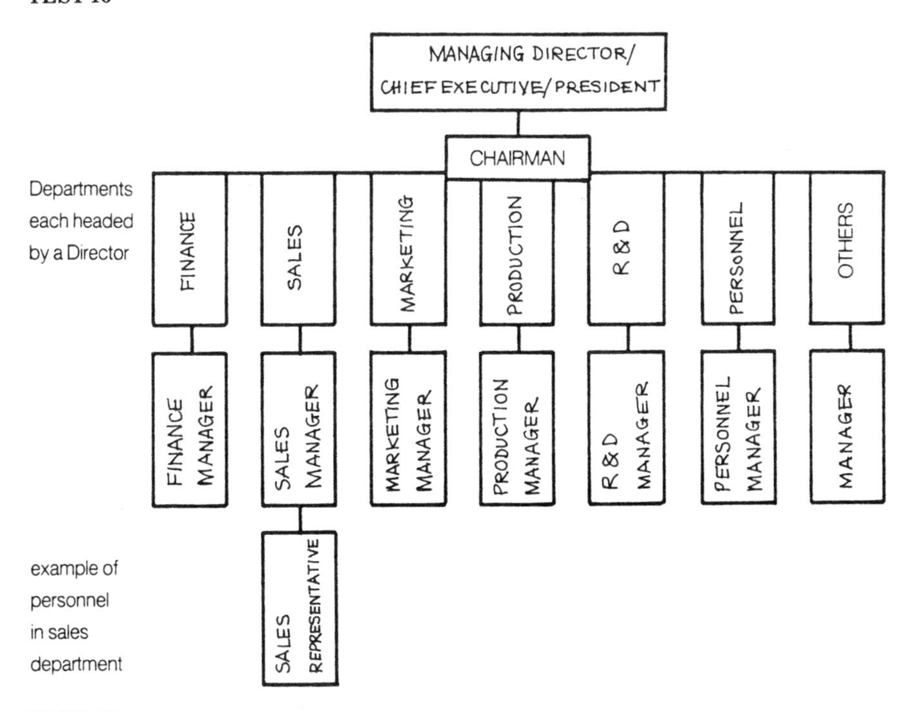

TEST 17

1 a
2 c
3 c
4 b
5 a
6 b
7 a
8 b
9 c
10 c

TEST 18

1 branch office
2 premises
3 location
4 rent
5 transport
6 conditions
7 fire
8 safety
9 appointed
10 hold stock
11 Head Office

TEST 19

1 personnel functions
2 Advertisements
3 Applicants
4 forms
5 chosen
6 short list
7 square pegs
8 round holes
9 interview
10 employment
11 holiday
12 pay
13 promotion
14 references

TEST 20

Across
2 join
4 argue
5 guards
6 point
7 strategy
8 issues
11 compromise

Down
1 deadlock
3 negotiation
4 agree
7 strike
9 settled
10 position
12 offer
13 refer

TEST 21

1 specification
2 freight/loading
3 charges
4 payment
5 delivery
6 letter of credit
7 penalty
8 invoked
9 substandard
10 late
11 reclaim
12 parties
13 arbitration
14 terms

TEST 22

1 profit
2 loss
3 cash-flow
4 market
5 sales
6 expenditure
7 capital
8 gross
9 net
10 overheads

TEST 23

1 a
2 c
3 b
4 b
5 c
6 a
7 b
8 a
9 c
10 a

TEST 24

1 merger
2 takeover
3 dawn raid
4 trade unions
5 bottom line
6 share price
7 management buyout
8 redundancies
9 redeployment
10 early retirement

TEST 25

1 a
2 c
3 a
4 b
5 c
6 b
7 a
8 a
9 c
10 a

TEST 26

1 sales
2 stock
3 tax
4 production
5 VAT
6 growth
7 cash
8 credit
9 creditors
10 debtors

TEST 27 See pages 88–9

TEST 28

1 **i** Bureau de Change
2 **j** cashier
3 **e** cash dispenser
4 **f** credit cards
5 **g** charge cards
6 **b** cheque book
7 **a** bank statement
8 **c** cheque guarantee card
9 **h** standing order

TEST 29

1 Bank of England
2 shares
3 Stock Exchange
4 stock
5 bull
6 bear
7 bond
8 bearer
9 asset
10 base rate

TEST 30

1 interest
2 exchange
3 VAT
4 bank
5 Dow Jones
6 FT
7 Nikkei Dow
8 current
9 open; close
10 draw

TEST 31

1 fixed
2 working
3 profit
4 balance
5 takeover
6 bought
7 post
8 books
9 delivery
10 advice

TEST 32

1 ApplicatioN
2 StatuS
3 SettlemenT
4 CrediT
5 DebiT
6 NotE
7 DiscounT
8 Pro formA
9 RaisE
10 BalancE

TEST 33

1 credit note
2 debit note
3 account
4 letter of credit
5 bill of lading
6 cost, insurance and freight
7 free on board
8 cost and freight
9 documents against acceptance
10 documents against payment

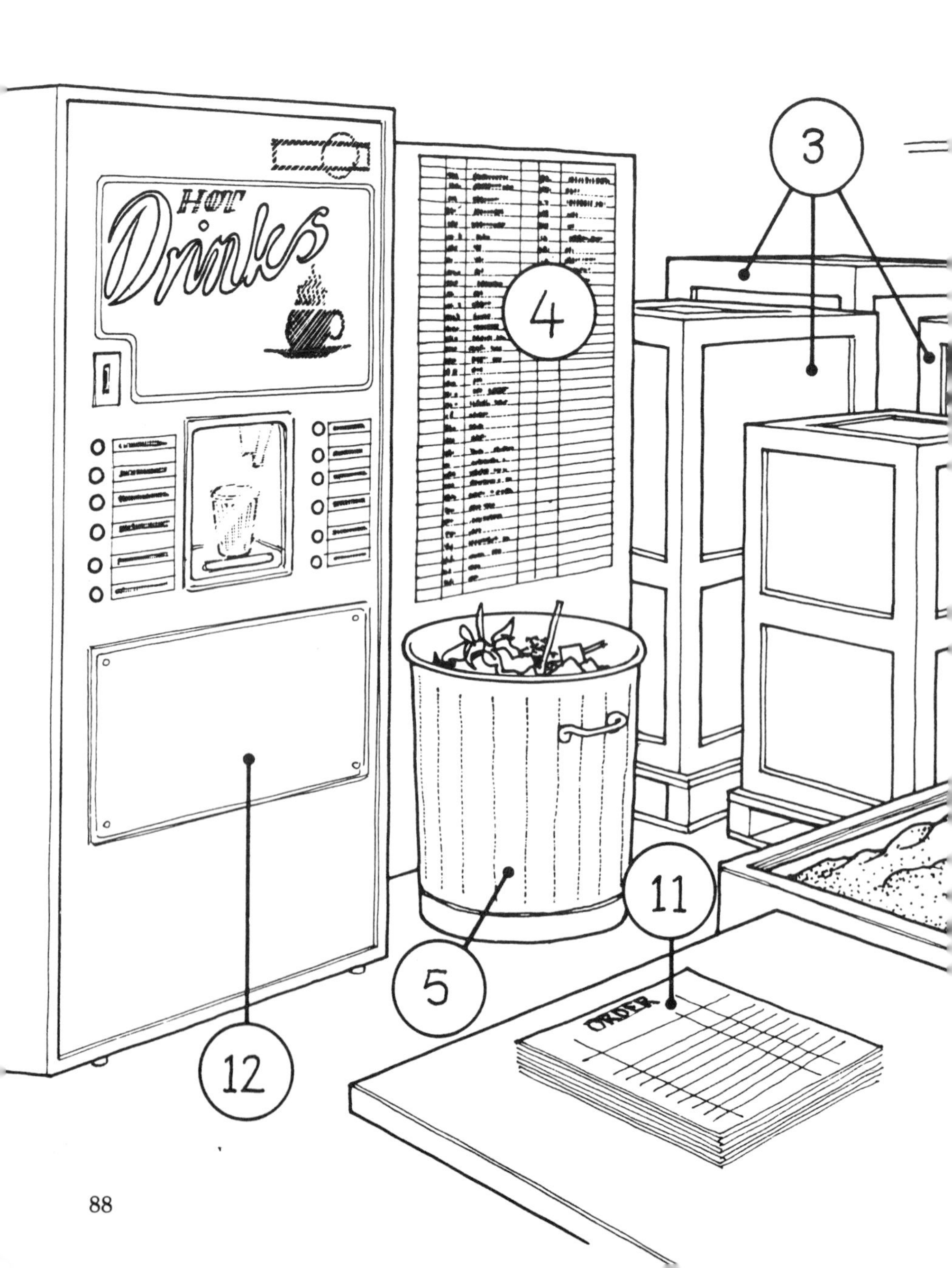
HOT
Drinks
3
4
5
11
12
ORDER

1
9
10
FRAGILE
6
8
2
7
TO

TEST 34

1 salary
2 wages
3 remuneration
4 adjust
5 return (on investment)
6 numbered
7 profit (margin)
8 expenses
9 account rendered
10 credit terms

TEST 35

1 policy
2 brokers
3 rates
4 risks
5 average
6 particular
7 special
8 floating
9 open
10 marine

TEST 36

1 **b** Directors
2 **a** venture
3 **b** return
4 **c** investment
5 **a** fixed
6 **c** variable
7 **b** cash flow
8 **a** profit and loss
9 **c** securities
10 **c** insurance adjusters
11 **a** stocks and shares
12 **b** takeover bid

TEST 37

Part A
1 bookkeeping
2 company
3 debtor
4 creditor
5 current
6 shares
7 dividend
8 profit
9 net
10 interest
11 statement
12 capital

Part B Opposite

TEST 38

1 accounts
2 auditors
3 books
4 reconcile
5 invoices/receipts
6 receipts/invoices
7 stocks
8 write down
9 depreciate
10 VAT
11 public
12 Exchange
13 Companies
14 annual
15 firms

TEST 39

1 Director
2 agent
3 reps
4 promotion
5 territory
6 appoint
7 open
8 credit-worthy
9 fax
10 forms

TEST 40 See pages 92–3

B U T S E R E T N I X A Y
P O B Q C A L T R E N U O
C M O H K R C A P I T A L
O C A K L D E B T O R I T
M S Y W K D L F E N P D U
P C U R R E N T P A B I L
A C S H A R E S Y M O V A
N D E Z L N X P R O F I T
Y P T E Q T R L I Y Z D P
R O T I D E R C X N T E H
E L S W A D E R T L G N S
S T A T E M E N T E A D F

6
2
5

7
10
8
4
12
9
11
1
3

TEST 41

1 sols raeled – loss leader
2 rutrnoev – turnover
3 kocts tnlcoor – stock control
4 aihnc – chain
5 icysretu – security
6 utsciond – discount
7 wrlahesole – wholesaler
8 hsovadeer – overheads
9 nidedmaml – middleman
10 hacs dna cryra – cash and carry

TEST 42

1 Marketing
2 promotion
3 Advertisements
4 exhibitions
5 media
6 market
7 budgets
8 copy
9 copy-writer
10 designer
11 set up
12 trade magazines
13 Trade
14 Commerce
15 price sensitivity
16 controls

TEST 43

Cartoon	Correct Caption
1	i
2	e
3	h
4	g
5	b
6	d
7	c
8	f
9	j
10	a

TEST 44

1 c
2 b
3 b
4 b
5 c
6 a
7 a
8 b
9 b
10 a
11 c
12 c

TEST 45

1 order no.
2 Date
3 Your ref./Our ref.
4 Quantity
5 Catalogue/item no.
6 Description
7 Unit cost
8 Total cost
9 Total
10 Packing
11 Marks
12 Delivery address
13 discounts
14 Authorised signature

TEST 46

1 EC – European Community
2 L/C – letter of credit
3 B/L – bill of lading
4 c.i.f – cost, insurance and freight
5 c. and f. – cost and freight
6 B/E – bill of exchange
7 D/P – documents against payment
8 D/A – documents against acceptance (of a bill of exchange)
9 sp.ex. – special export price
10 f.o.b. – free on board

TEST 47

1 bonded
2 sight
3 consular
4 first (of) exchange
5 freight
6 exporting
7 importing
8 consignment
9 free
10 insurance

TEST 48

1 exporting
2 imports
3 foreign
4 customs
5 invoices
6 certificates
7 export
8 agents
9 stock(s)
10 profit margin
11 commission
12 market research

TEST 49

1 cargo
2 manifest
3 consignments
4 documents
5 Excise
6 forwarding
7 services
8 shipping
9 cleared
10 destination

TEST 50

1 documentation
2 transport
3 stencilled
4 licence
5 declaration
6 ex works
7 customs
8 present
9 bill of lading
10 pro forma